D0934448

DISCARD

TALK:
CONVERSATIONS WITH
WILLIAM GOLDING

Jack I. Biles

TALK:

CONVERSATIONS WITH
WILLIAM GOLDING

Foreword by
William Golding

Harcourt Brace Jovanovich, Inc.
New York

823.9
B

Copyright © 1970 by Jack I. Biles
All rights reserved.
No part of this publication may be reproduced
or transmitted in any form or by any means,
electronic or mechanical, including photocopy, recording,
or any information storage and retrieval system,
without permission in writing from the publisher.
First edition
ISBN 0–15–187986–9
Library of Congress Catalog Card Number: 73–117570
Printed in the United States of America

For
Edith

newcomb - 12-1-70 - 3.97

Contents

Foreword

Some seven or eight years ago, when I was carting my wares round American universities, I had a sudden glimpse of what modern technology might come to mean for us all. I had lectured and was led away afterwards to meet faculty members and students. Since conversation is always easier than lecturing, this was a period of comparative placidity, when I was cheerful and relaxed. I answered questions with the euphoria of a man who has leapt yet another fence in a long race and can even see the finishing post. I was colloquial and witty; or, at least, those round me seemed to think so, laughing, as they balanced their cups of coffee. At last the party broke up; and just as I was about to leave, a young man appeared at the door, walked straight towards me, ignored me, bent down, extracted a tape recorder from beneath the seat I had just vacated, and disappeared through the door again. Now the most depressing aspect of this episode was not the tape recorder—since I was used to seeing them wherever I went—but the look in the eye of the young man who owned it. He was on the job. His eyes were set. His jaw and, indeed, his course were set. He had just the look of a man going busily down to the river for a bucket of water. I had not seen him before, and I have not seen him again; but I have no doubt that he went on collecting buckets of water from ponds, streams, rivulets, perhaps even the occasional Mississippi.

I suppose there must be moments when this young man meets people face to face; but, at the time, I was overcome by a dreadful vision of him surrounded by, wrapped up in, miles of tape from which rasp out the colorless, the dead leavings of a social occasion; and these leavings go beyond worthlessness into debit, when the listener was no part of the occasion itself. The young man was like those travelers who see only the view finder of a camera and end with so many photographs they have not time to examine them all—thus passing an expensive fortnight in seeing nothing whatsoever. Wittgenstein declared that a part of "Meaning" is the method used to convey it; and since a taped conversation cannot include the flash of an eye, a shrug, a gesture, it has about the same relationship to the total meeting, the *intercourse*, as its fossilized footprints have to a diplodocus. The young man who tried to catch an occasion at which he was not present, took away, so to speak, a fossilized impression of my social footprints—and much good may that do him.

Now this is one of the increasing horrors of our society. The moment leaves a permanent yet incomplete record behind it; and sometimes, may not our footprints be the casual, fortuitous, stumbling ones we would rather forget? When I multiply that young man and his secreted tape recorder by the number of my possible eavesdroppers in the United States of America alone, my inward ear hears myself baaing like a thousand sheep, clucking, braying, drooling the inconsequential and inconsistent. Fashion in books changes as quickly as fashion in clothes, and possibly today I could pass through an

American university without being noticed; but if anything could keep me away in something like terror, it is the thought that, during the last seven years, technology has swept ahead of us—and who knows now what weapons of distortion and offense the student has at his disposal?

There is, however, this consolation for the writer. Like the foolish traveler's too complete record of where he has been, the writer's detritus—whether it be letters, tapes, films, notes, diaries, scribbles, blots, doodles—is multiplying far faster than the scholars who find a career in sorting it. For the scholar has to undergo a long, professional training which puts off all but the toughest, whereas the writer needs only a pen, a piece of paper, a little wit, and a large slice of luck. Let us hope that we who have these four requirements can contrive to bog down scholarship in the sheer mass of material, until the political antics of humanity, or some natural catastrophe, deals finally with the lot.

Now having got that diatribe off my chest, I had better say something about the present book. The reader may object that I am inconsistent in agreeing to its publication. He is quite right. I am. But the reader may not be acquainted with Professor Biles, who is a warm and persuasive friend of mine and one to whom I have always found it quite impossible to say "no." He has pursued his objective with a relentlessness and a determination worthy of a far better cause; and the value of that cause—alas!—is for the reader to judge.

Yet I console myself with the thought that I am a professional writer; and a professional writer does not have to be a professional anything else. You would not require him to run a four-minute mile. Nor should you expect him to be coherent and consistent in answering questions off the cuff. He has his human rights like anyone else; and one of those rights is to be dull, discursive, and muddled, like the rest of his fellows. The expert conversationalist, the expert debater—these should be taped, rather than the creative writer. For the writer does his work elsewhere than in conversation—though as a novelist I would not deny that good stuff may erupt in talk.

Here, then, are traces of a conversation between friends. The warmth, the wine, the laughter are missing. So is the pressure of personality, the amiability of friendship. Most of all, what is missing is the sense of time flying, of spontaneity, of a moment snatched out of the air for a joke, then gone forever. But not quite gone. Those moments remain here, frozen relics of themselves, awaiting such thaw as the warmth of reading may provide.

WILLIAM GOLDING

TALK:
CONVERSATIONS WITH
WILLIAM GOLDING

"Ideas versus People":
Science Fiction

Biles: Kingsley Amis has a little book called *New Maps of Hell.* Do you remember this book?

Golding: Yes.

Biles: He says that Huxley, Orwell, and William Golding —in a rather different sense—take occasional trips into science fiction. Now I take it that he means *The Inheritors* and *Lord of the Flies.*

Golding: No, no. He might mean *Envoy Extraordinary,* which is another book I wrote.

Biles: Yes, he could mean *Envoy Extraordinary.* When you wrote these books, you didn't think of them as science fiction, and you don't now think of them so?

Golding: No, not in the least. They seem to me to be just the kind of straightforward things that people want to write, in the circumstances they find themselves in. I mean—how shall we put it?—after all, *Lord of the Flies* was simply what it seemed sensible for me to write after the war, when everybody was thanking God they weren't Nazis. And I'd seen enough and thought enough to realize that every single one of us could be Nazis; you take, for example, this bust-up in England over colored people—there were colored people in some suburban part of one of our cities; there really was a bust-up over this—and you take the South, of North America, where you have a regular bust-up over Negroes. And take anybody's history, what it comes to is this: that Nazi Germany was a particular kind of boil which burst in 1939 or 1940 or whenever it was. That was only the same kind of inflamed spot we all of us suffer from, and so I took English boys and said, "Look. This could be you." This is really what that book comes to.

As far as *The Inheritors* goes . . . One of the big books in my youth—for me, as for most of the people of my generation, I suspect—was Wells' *Outline of History,* which was not only humanist, but also had a kind of furtive optimism which can't really be expressed nowadays, because we've got rid of it. But it was almost a nineteenth-century kind of optimism, to the effect that all you had to do was to make bigger and bigger façades in Manchester and everybody would end up by being all perfect. You see, there was some kind of social perfectibility in man, which there *may* be, but I didn't see it at that time; therefore, I went back into Wells' book and looked at the premises that he was using and decided I didn't agree with them. So I stood them on their heads and tried to show that they would be the same sort of thing.

This is more or less what it comes to. As far as I am concerned, this is not science fiction. To me, this is dealing with things which are very germane to my own education and to my own experience. I don't think this is science fiction at all.

Biles: But the problem depends upon some sort of definition of science fiction; in other words, what do *you* mean? You say "science fiction." You don't think these books are science fiction; that means that you have some sort of a notion, some sort of definition, of what science fiction *is*. What is it?

Golding: Well, it's irresponsibility, is it not, really? It's playing with ideas that don't actually matter, or, if the ideas matter, you engage them to people that don't matter. In other words, if the idea is important enough, then what you have [for characters] is paper cutouts, because you can't show me any science fiction which is post-Wells, I would suspect, in which people matter one damn. There is always a beautiful blonde who is lugged in, because you must have a bit of sex; and you can't tell the difference between Professor This and Professor That or Joe This or Joe That—they're all either "goodies" or "baddies." In a sense, it's the same as a western, is it not? When you can't introduce character, because, if you do, the story becomes a real one and, therefore, black and white are invariably mixed up.

Biles: All serious readers would say that *Brave New World* is an example of the science-fiction novel, and they would say that it is much superior to run-of-the-mill. Now the difference between *Brave New World* and, say, *Point Counter Point*, the only real difference, is that *Brave New World* is set at a remote time in the future—the twenty-sixth century A.D. or the sixth century A.F., "after Ford." There are no *real characters* in *Point Counter Point*, are there? Huxley is notorious for his personae being not characters, but merely mouthpieces for ideas. So, again, what is the real difference?

Notice, for example, that one of the adverse criticisms which have been made against your books, by certain commentators, is that you don't sufficiently characterize, which, if this were true, would square with what you just said, that where the idea is the main thing in a book, the author must diminish character because, if character is pointed up, the reader becomes interested in the individuals and loses sight of the ideas. Hence, you would agree with that principle. What, then, really is the difference between *Brave New World* and *Point Counter Point?*

Golding: Well, I would have to enter a caveat here, and that would simply be to say that if my characters aren't interesting, then this is my fault.

You can look at this whole question from two points of view. You can say, "Well, obviously, *Brave New World* doesn't bother about characters, because it is concerned entirely with ideas." On the other hand, Huxley was a man who was much more interested in ideas than in people; therefore, though he tries, I think, in *Point Counter Point* to present a broad canvas of society as he knew it, in fact he is less successful there even with his ideas than he is with his characters. In effect, he is a natural writer of *Brave New World*, but an unnatural writer of *Point Counter Point*. Can you see at all what I'm getting at here?

Biles: I don't quite know what you mean by "natural" here.

Golding: Well, I mean his instinctive preference was for the novel of ideas. And, although in *Point Counter Point* I think he really, genuinely tried to start with people, nevertheless, he superimposes on them a scheme, so that, in fact, although perhaps no over-all idea except that of ultimate pessimism emerges—well, perhaps not so much in *Point Counter Point*—but although he starts with character in one novel, he still begins to superimpose ideas on it, because his natural function is to be a kind of pessimistic Bunyan.

Biles: He is really an essayist and not a novelist?

Golding: I don't know. Perhaps he is an allegorist, or perhaps he is just simply an ideas man. I wouldn't know. All I'm trying to say here is that it is surely not the function of the critic to say so much what the difference is between *Point Counter Point* and *Brave New World* as it is the function of the critic to say what sort of man Huxley was, why it was that he could write more successfully *Brave New World* than he could *Point Counter Point*—which, I think, is what happened. *Point Counter Point* might perhaps be *War and Peace*, but it isn't, because Huxley is not Tolstoy.

Now what you're really asking me, in a sense, is to define myself and say whether I'm not really an ideas man rather than a character man. I think this may have been so; I hope it won't always be so, but I think it is probably true. I think it is probably true that I'm more interested in ideas than in people.

Biles: But I understood, when he began to talk about this, that you were saying that in *Lord of the Flies* you intended to characterize. Your intention was to create real little boys; you were writing about people, not simply about ideas, as Huxley presumably was in *Brave New World*, and so it is a matter of whether you succeeded or not. In any case, you intended to do it.

Golding: Yes, I think this is true. And this goes back to my other point: that I think what one has to say about a writer is "Such was his intention. What kind of shot did he make of it?" If people say I didn't manage to characterize, well, then, this is my defect.

Biles: Notwithstanding, your intention was to characterize in *Lord of the Flies*; is the same true of all your books?

Golding: If you can think of it as a needle going either plus or minus, I think it's probably true to say of my books that the needle tends to quiver over towards ideas rather than towards people. I think this is a bad thing and, if I were a critic, I would put that down as my basic defect, or the basic defect of my books.

Biles: That is to say, if one felt that you failed in this respect *in a given book?*

Golding: I wouldn't even say that. I would say it as an overall criticism, and anyone who writes books like that, however lofty and good his ideas may be—and I think my ideas *are* good—still has a defect, if the ideas can't be shown through people who convince. If critics find my characters unconvincing, then I've failed to that extent. I think a book should have both real people and real ideas—if you can *have* a real idea. But it should have the two, and Huxley hasn't got the real two in *Brave New World.* If people tell me I haven't got the real two in *Lord of the Flies,* or anything else, then I have to accept this.

Biles: Of course, there is another side to this: there are critics who argue that you do characterize. I simply was quoting, not specifically, the critics who said "no."

Golding: I would agree with them.

Biles: Would you? In general?

Golding: I would agree with them in pretty specific terms, I think. After all, you can't have your cake and eat it: if you are dependent upon, if your motivation in a sense *is,* an idea, then it can't be character. And I think this is a bad thing.

As a specific example, take *Pilgrim's Progress.* Well, no one would claim, "Here are great characters." On the other hand, if you take *Henry IV,* you can see a man who started off with an idea, a medieval idea, a morality or Vice. Falstaff is a Vice,

I think, when he starts in Shakespeare's mind, but Falstaff gets away from him; Falstaff becomes a character, because Shakespeare had this *God-given* aptitude for really, in a sense, evaluating the given nature of man. And, although Shakespeare starts with his Vice, he ends up with a character whom everybody is supposed to despise and hate, but whom it takes a very rigidly moral man to dislike at all, by the time Shakespeare finishes. You find that in the end Henry V himself is much more like a medieval Virtue than he is like a man, but the medieval Vice, Falstaff, is become a man. The tragedy of *Henry IV, Part II*, is the fall of Falstaff.

Biles: Isn't that heartbreaking?

Golding: It *is* heartbreaking, and, so far, understandable. Now I think this is perfectly true: there are two sorts of writers. There are people who have this genuine attachment to the . . . not the human condition so much as to the human being, and I think that Dickens and Shakespeare and Homer —and almost anybody you can mention who is really great— do really deal with this basic kind of thing that goes along the arteries. It doesn't go into the brain, hardly goes into the brain at all. It has some kind of basic connection with the value of the human being. I think this is the most important literary thing—or artistic thing, if you like. I would wish, if I could be, to be that kind of writer; but, if people tell me not, well, then, I would agree, because I suspect not. Can you see at all what I'm getting at? It's fine to start off with a medieval morality, but some writers end up with human beings. Others, alas, start with human beings and end up with medieval moralities; this is a very bad way of doing it.

Biles: Of course. But you are citing extremes. Take, for instance, *The Middle Age of Mrs. Eliot.* There is some difficulty, it takes a certain amount of professorializing, to say what the ideas in that book are; but if ever there were a characterization—a fully realized, rounded, whole, believable woman—it's Meg Eliot.

Golding: Yes.

Biles: Well, it doesn't necessarily follow from the fact of characterization that *The Middle Age of Mrs. Eliot* is a better book, in whatever terms you want to use, than, say, *Lord of the Flies*.

Golding: Well, then, you must say whatever terms you are going to use, what it is all about. I wouldn't know how to answer to this; all I can say is that *Lord of the Flies*, I think, made the point I wanted it to make, and I would have to leave it at that.

Think of *Don Quixote*, for example. Now there you have a case in point, have you not? Here is Cervantes, who sets out to rib medieval romance and ends up with the man of the next three hundred years, more or less. Well, I don't think, therefore, that it is possible in our particular terms—dealing as we do in matters of years and not centuries—to say whether Meg Eliot has any ideas behind her. It is much more important that she should be a thorough person than that she should be a thorough idea, do you see? And so, in these terms, I would regard that as more important than *Lord of the Flies*, although the idea in *Lord of the Flies* is good. But what we are concerned with is people and not ideas. I think that perhaps ideas ought to take second place.

Piggy

Golding: Ah, well, Piggy is a scientist. He is a technocrat. He was meant to be a scientist.

Biles: I imagine you would term it a kind of empathy of rationalism, but I have a note here about Piggy, and I'm a little unhappy that you said what you just said, because . . .

Golding: Because you admire a scientist as being . . .

Biles: No, I do not!

Golding: You have been brought up carefully.

Biles: I do not. No, sir. I'm a humanist.

Golding: Are you really?

Biles: Yes, indeed. Deliver me from the Great God Science. I mean Science is H. G. Wells, to use a term offensive to you.

Golding: But he is an Admirable Novelist, a Great Man.

Biles: Seriously, though, I have been bothered by a certain patronizing air of critics toward Piggy. They dislike him, that is, the little boy himself. Even Frank Kermode refers to Piggy with such words as "dull" and "practical." People rather scornfully call him "scientific." I am not sure that I entirely agree with this view of Piggy, and your describing him condescendingly as "a scientist" caught me with my guard momentarily down. After all, you're the man who called him "wise."

Golding: I didn't call him wise.

Biles: You bloody well did.

Golding: Ralph did.

Biles: No, sir. I am not going to have that . . .

Golding: Who wrote this?

Biles: . . . because the very end of the book is not dialogue.

Golding: "True, wise friend called Piggy."

Biles: That's right. "True," which does not square really with these contemptuous things that people say about Piggy. And "wise." "Wise."

Golding: How shall I put it? It is a technical mistake in that case, if you thought of it as *my* view of Piggy. I am dealing there with . . . I am, up to a point, inside Ralph's skull, and he is weeping for the end of innocence and the darkness of man's heart and the fall through the air of the true, wise friend called Piggy. Those are things seen entirely from inside Ralph. Nobody else can see them. And, he should be weeping for Simon.

Biles: Yes, he should be.

Golding: But he's not.

Biles: Well, he doesn't understand.

Golding: He doesn't understand. He understands Piggy. He understands Piggy, and he thinks him wise. Piggy isn't wise. Piggy is short-sighted. He is rationalist. My great curse, you understand, rationalism—and, well, he's that. He's naïve, short-sighted, and rationalist, like most scientists.

Biles: But the difference is that Piggy is *right*.

Golding: Ah, well, then I have no more to say.

Biles: Isn't he?

Golding: Well, how is he right? He surely shows his complete ignorance of the situation, when he talks about acting like a crowd of kids, just when they are acting like a crowd of grownups. And he is the one who wants his auntie there and thinks that people would meet and discuss and the rest of it. He's an innocent; he's a complete innocent. He is like scientists, who really think they're getting somewhere in real, genuine, human terms. They are getting more complicated—and, personally, I find it fascinating, the whole thing. I am quite sure, if I had cancer, they probably would do better for me than they would have ten years ago. It is fine, but it's naïve. It doesn't even touch the human problem. Piggy never gets anywhere near coping with anything on that island at all. He dismisses the beast, he dismisses the beastie, he says there aren't such things as ghosts, not understanding that the whole of society is *riddled* with ghosts. It may be their parents' ghosts, but it's still ghosts. They're riddled with them. Piggy understands society less than almost anyone there at all. He's a scientist.

Biles: Certainly, he is practical, but . . .

Golding: He is that sort of practical—he's a practical scientist.

Biles: I want Piggy to be a little more than that, just a little more.

Golding: Ah, well, you're a sentimentalist.

Biles: Well, yes, I am. I hope in the best, not in the worst, sense. We started with that premise. But, at the same time, Piggy says that they have got to have some kind of semblance of order. Piggy wants Ralph to protect him from Jack, which is understandable. Notwithstanding the discreditable aspects of Piggy, it seems to me that there is a little more to Piggy than the objectors give him. In the end, most of the things he says are right; they may not go far enough, they may not touch the heart of the problem, but they are at least right, aren't they?

Golding: They're righter than most. There are degrees of rightness, aren't there? There is the furthest degree that anybody on the island goes, which is to go up the mountain and see what there is at the top. That is Simon, who is understood by nobody, naturally enough. There is Ralph, who has some idea of law and order, and there is Piggy, who realizes that what they need more than anything else is rescue, and, second to that, shelter, which, after all, Ralph does realize, too. Piggy has a certain basic technological ability in that he sees roughly what can't be done, what is impossible. He doesn't see what's possible there, much. No, I would say Piggy ought to wear a white coat—one of these long white lab coats—and ramble round the island, probably writing papers about this, that, or t'other, and ending up at Los Alamos. If I gave him more than that, then I'm glad to see it's one of those cases where Falstaff got out of the situation of being a medieval Vice.

Biles: I am haggling over Piggy, in my own mind, and I'm going to keep haggling. I'm not quite ready to settle for this.

Golding: Well, you must remember I haven't read the book, anyway, since I wrote it. I remember some key sentences. The last one, which I thought of first, more or less. Any others? Oh, I remember the interview between the pig and Simon. Apart from that, very little, except the general shape.

"Your Own Books"

Because Golding was forty-three when Lord of the Flies *was published, a BBC "Monitor" interviewer observed in 1959, "This seems rather late to start writing." Golding responded, "I didn't start writing when I was forty; I had been writing ever since I was seven. I suppose you can say I've been effectively writing since I was thirty-five. I published my first book, or had my first book published, a book of verse, when I was nine-teen* [actually, when he was twenty-three—published October 30, 1934]. *I'll say very little more about that; I just want to forget that one. Nobody knows anything about it. And then, out of the rest, you've got to take five years for the war, in the navy, and ten years, perhaps, learning to write by imitating other people and learning very late that, of course, I was merely writing other people's novels instead of my own. And it was not until I was thirty-seven, I suppose, that I grasped the great truth that you've got to write your own books and nobody else's. Then everything followed from that."*

Biles: Do you remember the professor in one of Louisa May Alcott's books—*Little Women,* I guess—advising Jo to quit writing foolish romances about kings and castles and other things that she did not know about? He said for her to go home and write about what she did know about. It sounds somewhat like Sir Philip Sidney. Good advice, wouldn't you say?

Golding: I don't know. I think it depends somewhat upon the person, doesn't it? I don't think it is altogether good advice.

Biles: How do you mean?

Golding: Some of the fun of writing is writing what you didn't think you could. This is a curious kind of thing, a book which is impossible, anyway. After all, I have never been drowned, and I have never been flung up on a rock—never been to hell, in so many words. And therefore this is anti-Louisa May Alcott stuff I'm talking.

Biles: I see.

Golding: Writing is not reportage, but imagination. Therefore, I don't think you ever write about what you know about. You write about what you guess about and what you imagine about. This is one way of doing it.

You can be Anthony Trollope and write about things you do know about, but that is another kind of writing. Or you can be Louisa May Alcott. She knew about this New England Providence, this sort of family, this sort of house, and all the rest of it; so she chose to write that way, and that is why she made her professor say what he did. But if I had had the handling of that professor, I would have made him say, "Look, my dear girl, the trouble with you is, you are writing the book that you *ought* to write—these fantastic adventures —but you just can't do it. So, what had you best do? Just get back to the tiny little book you *can* write."

Biles: I still don't think that you really are disagreeing, in a special sense. Here we are back to semantics again. Perhaps it is not so much what you know about as it is what you care about, what you are concerned with. I grant you haven't been drowned and I grant you haven't been literally in hell, but you have been in the navy, you have seen men who were drowned, you are concerned about hell, you have thought about it, so that, perhaps, we are really arguing about "know about" and "intellectually concerned with."

Golding: Yes. It's not a straight A or B, is it?

Biles: Let me ask you to say something about two things. I have had a couple of utterly delightful visits with Angus Wilson since I last saw you and, offhand, I can't recall whether he said both these things to me or whether I read them. Angus said, nevertheless, and this is a quotation, "*All* novelists are trying to convince the reader that he is seeing society as a whole." Unfortunately, there is an ambiguous reference of the pronoun, so that it is unclear whether "he" is the novelist or the reader, unless Angus wants it both ways.

Golding: I'd think it is *absolutely true* in Angus' position: both ways, no ambiguities, both the reader and the writer. About me, I wouldn't know. I have never even considered this question.

Biles: He said *all* novelists. Angus says also—which, in one way, comes palpably close to you and, in another, perhaps it doesn't at all—that the main responsibility of modern man is facing what he is—that pins you—and assessing, facing, the Freudian motivations of his actions. I doubt whether you would accept the latter, but you do agree, don't you, that the main responsibility of modern man is facing what he is?

Golding: Yes.

Biles: What about this business of the "Freudian motivations of his actions"?

Golding: There I have to make this admission that I had to make all the way round campuses in America which shocked all the young men—and the young women even more. I have never read any Freud, you see; so I don't know. It makes it very difficult indeed. I don't know what one would say of facing the "Freudian motivations of his actions." I don't think one has to lug Freud in there. I think one can do without this and say "facing the motivations of his actions." One has just as much access to one's make-up as Freud had to his and I think almost as much to other people's motivations as Freud had to other people's. I wouldn't see why we'd have to bring Freud in here.

I suggested at one point that it would make a happy little geometric pattern, of the sort so dear to the academic literary mind, if Golding would confess a deliberate symbolic use of the four elements of ancient Greek atomic theory, because of the prominent and reiterated emphasis upon earth, air, fire, and water in all his work. He dexterously and wittily avoided the bait. He courteously shunted our talk aside, without the least indication that he recognized that I was as heedless and foolish as I was.

Golding: If you ask me about the four elements, all I can say is that the Greeks were faced with fire and earth and air and water; they saw a lot of them, because they were human beings who were living. I have seen a lot of fire, a lot of water, a lot of earth, and breathed a lot of air. I have just as natural a relationship with them as anybody else has. If the elements are in the books, it is because this is what our life consists in.

Biles: So it is a question of fundamentals, rather than of symbols. Or it is really both.

Golding: Oh, now, what are symbols? Now you tell me.

Biles: We can play textbook.

Golding: All right, let's play textbook.

Biles: All right. The best elementary introduction to poetry that I know makes a very clear distinction which, I think, despite its oversimplicity, is yet sound. The discrimination made is that the image means what it is and the symbol means what it is and something else besides. It is a very simple dichotomy, but I think it is useful and meaningful.

Golding: In that case, I would suspect that everything is symbolic. Is that not so?

Biles: Well . . .

Golding: This mainly, not perhaps, this is the great catch: is it in the nature of the thing in itself or in the nature of the human being who has the perception? In other words, is fire symbolic in itself or do I see it as symbolic because I am a human being using a particular network?

Biles: We would say—now wouldn't we?—that fire, to fire, is not symbolic; that fire is inanimate; that fire does not know it burns; that it is nonconscious; hence, any symbolism which fire might have would obviously be in our heads and not in the fire.

Golding: This is what Piggy would say, mark you, when he had gone to college and then had gone on to a doctorate, which would inevitably be concerned in some way or other with his experiences on the island. This is how Piggy would explain the fires on the island, and I wonder whether he would be right or not. How would Simon explain them?

Biles: I know you have been over this fifty times, but I'd like to be clear. I have made the point several times that people had better pay attention to what you say about the sources of your books, because you have said many times that they have relatively little genesis outside yourself. And you freely acknowledge and point to them, like *The Coral Island* and *Lord of the Flies*. James R. Baker in his book makes a great deal of Greek literature. I can see this, of course; for example, the Prometheus business in *Pincher Martin*, and so on. There is a strong element, certainly. Would you say that the principal literary influence upon you is Greek drama, history, mythology, and so on? Do you think that is the major influence on you?

Golding: You are talking about literature?

Biles: Yes.

Golding: It ought to be. I would think the Aristotelian concept of tragedy is probably something that I have taken without really wondering in the Brechtian sense whether I should take it. In fact, I have been wondering more and more, lately, whether perhaps I haven't been too much concerned with the tragic hero and whether this isn't one of the reasons why my books lack a number of dimensions of reality. *Because* this is a highly specialized, highly stylized, very laudable, and youthful view of what a performance should be, what a dramatic act or an act of art, if you like, should be. But we don't really, any longer, make statues the way the Greeks made; so why should we take Aristotle's word for tragedy when we've got other—I'm talking now as a maker, you see. This is not a question of feeling or anything else, it is a question of technique. You want to do so and so; well, obviously, you have to have a tragic hero, who starts with a flaw and ends up at the bottom. I think I took that for granted, I just accepted that, perhaps less out of Aristotle than out of Greek tragedy itself, which is in a way a bond to Aristotle, isn't it? I think it is true that Greek literature really has been the *big* literary influence in my life, but I think that that may very well have come to an end, and so may I.

Comedy

In The Spectator *for July 7, 1961, Golding published an amusing essay about the woes and frustrations of the struggling young writer. He comments on the "trail of scribbled paper" which writers leave behind. Golding may keep some of his "scribbled paper," but he often burns it, a practice bound to grieve any scholar.*

Biles: Let me chide you.

Golding: What about?

Biles: This business about burning stuff. You mustn't *do* that.

Golding: Well, somebody once told me that there is a university somewhere in America which is so rich that on Sundays it puts up rockets, but on weekdays it buys the lunch bills and the train tickets and all the rest from authors. Now this is the university I've been looking for. If you come across it, just tell me. Apparently they have rows and rows and rows of green filing cabinets, in a basement where they are not going to be bombed, full of carnival hats.

Biles: You have previously said something to me about your dissatisfaction with everybody's thinking you're so bloody grim, and I must say that some of your essays, the funny ones, are absolutely screaming.

Golding: Well, thank you very much.

Biles: I am quite serious. The funniest thing I ever read in my life is that creative-writing thing ["Gradus ad Parnassum"] where you drag in Blake. [Golding chuckled.] I laughed till the tears ran down my cheeks.

Golding: Good.

Biles: You have written a handful of very funny things, and I was making a point that nobody ever has commented on this. The only thing they ever mention about anything funny is the very hard, bitter comedy. For example, in *Free Fall*, when Beatrice wets the floor the way Minnie had done in the school. They point to that and they say, "Look how bitter this all is." You have written a lot of funny things. Are you going to write more comic things? Don't you want to write comic things? Tell me about comedy.

Golding: Tell you about comedy. I think this is perhaps anti-Aristotelian, the point I'm really getting around to. A very old friend of mine said, some time ago, about six months ago, "There is a gap between you and your books." I said, "Well, hell, of course there is." Then, later on, Ann [Mrs. Golding] said, "The thing about your books is that you've never put all of yourself into them." And I thought to myself, walking along by that river down there [behind Ebble Thatch, Golding's home in Wiltshire], "What does this mean?" And then I thought, "Well, of course, this really goes along with my feeling that in a way I was a bit of a fool to take Aristotle for granted, that one should break away from that whole concept. There *is* room for a complete spread. There are obviously novels, or plays or whatever, in which the whole compass is there. This wouldn't do any *good*, but it would give, perhaps, a more valid impress of what it is like to be alive." You see, I laugh a lot.

Biles: You do indeed.

Golding: And it could be, in this great, grim universe I portray, that a tiny, little, rather fat man with a beard, in the middle of it laughing, is more like the universe than a gaunt man struggling up a rock.

Biles: You said, then, that you feel that you have left out a little comedy. Does this suggest that you ought to put some in?

Golding: No, it doesn't. I don't think it's a question of putting some in. I think it's a question of seeing that comedy and tragedy are . . .

Biles: Twins?

Golding: More than that. That's one of these damned literary metaphors. They're not twins; they are the same person. I can remember this: I was in a hospital during the war, and some man was brought in, and he was pretty well beat up, shot to pieces. They went and operated on him, and then they put him in this ward and he came round. He was coming round, and all the time he was coming round he was making terrific breathing noises, because he had a tube down his throat. Then this died down. And the noises were funny. This was the thing. And he was unconscious, you see. He wasn't suffering. People were giggling all round this ward.

Then the sister came in, or it may have been a nurse, and took this tube out and propped him up. He stopped making those noises and started making being-sick noises. The nurse hadn't got a basin with her and she rushed away. She came down these polished floors with this basin, and about five yards from the bed, she fell flat on her face. The basin flew through the air and landed right on this man's head and rang. Ding-g-g-g! Like that. And everybody in that ward—there were people bursting their stitches.

And of course I recognized this when I saw that film "The Great Chase," where everybody busts up cars and falls down cliffs and so on. A funny film, but, again, about pain and grief. Looking back, I was thinking to myself that there I was, sitting up in that bed or lying up in the bed, rather, and saying to myself, "What can one write about this ward?" Then this happened. And there was this complete comic situation, with the extraordinary thing, how the basin fell on the man's head. It sounded like a bell. I gave up writing for years after that.

Biles: The trouble is that people get a fixed idea about a writer, whoever he might be, and they read every subsequent work in the light of the fixed idea. I think there are genuinely funny things in the serious books you have written. Some of the plainly comic essays are hilarious. I wish you would write more of that kind. That essay you wrote about going across on . . . it must have been the *Queen Mary.*

Golding: "A Touch of Insomnia." It was the *Queen Elizabeth.*

Biles: Mary or *Elizabeth,* it is the same thing. This is so funny.

Golding: I meant it funny, but it's regarded as a profound bit of social criticism.

Funny War Stories

Biles: During the war you were in some way connected with Lord Cherwell's research establishment.

Golding: I went into the war as an ordinary seaman and, subsequently, went through for being an officer. On an examination, I remember, one of the answers was on the difference between a propellant and an explosive. I enjoyed this kind of thing, you see, and where they wanted an answer in about two sentences, I gave them three pages with graphs and things. The result was that I was suddenly whipped out of there and hurled into the middle of the country to a highly secret research establishment, which was under the direct control of one Professor Lindemann, who was scientific adviser to Churchill and who ultimately became Lord Cherwell.

I was there for very nearly a year, right in the middle of England, all dressed up as a naval officer and trying to invent things that would sink submarines. It was fantastic. I enjoyed a lot of it, made immense bangs.

Biles: What did you do in New York, when you were sent there? Was that part of the same thing?

Golding: I left the research establishment in this way. We were working at all times on this antisubmarine thing, and I was doing a lot of tests, scaled-down tests, with explosives.

One day I put a lot of detonators in my pocket and dropped a torch battery in with them and blew myself up. You see, when I came down and was fished out of hospital and gradually tidied up, I said, "Well, I will have my bangs in the appropriate places, and if anybody is going to blow me up, it can be somebody else."

I went to the Admiralty and said, "Send me back to sea, for God's sake, where there's peace." They said, "What would you like to do?" And I said that I had learnt an awful lot about explosives, and they said, "So has everybody else."

I wanted a small ship, because I didn't much care for big ones. They have so many people on them. I said, "What about mine sweeping?" They said, "Fine," and sent me to Scotland to learn about mine sweeping. When they had finished in Scotland, they sent me straight over to New York to wait while you built a mine sweeper out on Long Island. I sat there for, God knows, about six months, something of this order, till the mine sweeper was done, and then brought it back. But by that time the mine problem had been licked, and they were all ready for invading Europe.

So I said, "Look, this is a very dull job I'm doing; can I get a little closer to the coal face?" They said, "Yes, indeed you can." They asked what I knew about, and I said instantly, "Explosives." They said, "Well, the rocket is the thing." They put me in one of these damned rocket craft, and I finished the war. It was very interesting.

Biles: I know very little about rocket-launching craft. I gather that those craft were secret, anyway. Was the function a matter of running over and bombarding the coast and coming back and reloading, that kind of thing?

Golding: What you did was, for about twenty-four seconds, to keep up the kind of bombardment that couldn't be done any other way, because people could not load that fast. This soaked the coast just as the infantry were going in. When they hit the beaches, you had to lay this kind of pattern down in front of them. It looked terribly dramatic. I was most impressed with myself, but it was the safest job in the business, I'm glad to say.

Biles: About this affair you said was all misunderstood, your standing up on the bridge and grinning like a Cheshire cat?

Golding: This is literally true, and it's about the only thing I really remember vividly in the war. We had to go and invade the island of Walcheren, and we had no air support. We knew that the only thing that all the support craft could do, whilst everybody ashore was all inside concrete—we knew perfectly well what would happen—would be that we would have to steam up and down or in and out, looking fierce and heroic and getting sunk, while the army got ashore. I knew exactly what the situation was and I was very, very frightened. About dawn, I started to put a grin on my face because I thought, "Well, after all, this is the navy, and I'm in charge of this tin box"; so I grinned, just to show everybody that there was nothing to worry about.

I was so frightened that this grin got stuck on my face, and it went on all the morning. We got shot up and everything, everybody was throwing stuff in every direction, there were colossal bangs and cascades of water, and I couldn't get rid of my grin. My whole crew were going round muttering to each other and saying, "It can't be as bad as all that, because the Old Man is enjoying it."

Then there came one moment when we were just about to

do a real death-and-glory run, and I still couldn't get rid of my grin, but even my crew thought this was pretty grim, you see, and they still looked up and said, "You see the Old Man, he's still grinning, he's all for it, he likes this kind of thing." Then we got a signal canceling what would have been absolute nonsense—we were going to steam in all on our own, four miles from anybody else, right down the barrel of the gun.

We got a signal canceling this, you see, and I suddenly thought, "My God, I'm going to live," and my grin fell off. I couldn't do anything with my face. It just collapsed. The crew said, "Do you see that old bastard up there? When he learnt we weren't going in, he was disappointed!"

This is the funniest thing I remember about the war.

The War as Awakening

Biles: You said to me last spring that before the war you were a very naïve person. You said that, then, you believed in, I suppose, the perfectibility of man. You said you thought that you didn't believe what you heard about Nazi Germany. You thought that if we should establish a perfect social system, we would then, in effect, have perfect people.

Now you changed your mind during the war, and after the war you wrote *Lord of the Flies*. I want to ask you two things. One is, if you would, to be a little more specific about the changing of your mind during the war. The other I know very little about, but you wrote several novels after the war, novels of the kind which ordinarily would be termed "pot-boilers." They were novels which you wrote to *sell*. You said that you wrote what you thought people wanted to read, and it didn't come off.

Well, now, if you had a great reorientation during the war, why didn't you set right about writing *Lord of the Flies*? Why did you write the other novels? Was the reason purely economic?

Golding: No indeed, it wasn't economic. It was simply, I suppose, the fact that I didn't really believe I could bring it off. I thought that *you* may think these things and you think they're true, but they're not really what people are thinking about. They're not really what other people believe. This is a private idea of yours. It was only after I had written three books which nobody wanted to publish, and I can *understand* that, that I began to see.

I am a very late developer, you see. I have just about reached my adolescence, at the moment. In a sense, I—well, but that depends on how long one lasts. It's a good thing, I think, because it means everything gets stretched out and, therefore, you can take more time about thinking things. But the books I have written since the war are perhaps the things, if I had been someone else, I would have written between eighteen and twenty-two.

Biles: These are the unpublished books?

Golding: No, no, no, these are the ones I've written. Any man goes through this period of thinking what everybody else writes is what I ought to be writing, only I ought to be writing even *more so.*

I didn't really think, I didn't really believe, I had any capacity for communication with other people. I started by writing poetry, and my poetry is very bad. I never believed that anything more than poetry, or perhaps poetical dramas, is worth writing. It was only when I had written these books, which were what other people believed, that I came round to saying it's time that you wrote a book for yourself, because, obviously, nothing else is going to matter. It was just chance your arm on this thing; just write it. Then I wrote *Lord of the Flies,* which was things I had come to believe during the war.

This is, in a sense, a kind of adolescence, a feeling that one has specific *ideas* that have to be put over. Now, I'm not sure I believe that any more. I think I know far less now than I did after the war. This is what I mean when I say I'm a slow developer.

I believe one surely has to go through, after the period of knowing what one thinks, one surely has to go through a period of knowing what one does not think, of being astonished. If one ever comes through to really, finally knowing what one thinks, I don't know, but I am moving into a kind of position of seeing the ideas I had as the partial things they were. Therefore, I say my books have been written out of a kind of delayed adolescence.

But don't underestimate adolescence, delayed or not, because it is a time when you see things very clearly, and it could be that the ideas that I have written about are the right ideas to write about. But I'm not sure, if you're really going to be a writer, that they should be written about as ideas; perhaps they should be written about as people. After all, what is the good of having ideas, if there aren't any people?

My books, on the whole, I think, tend to lean towards the ideas being important and the people not. We have been through this before, but I think it is probably true. It is surely better to look at it the other way round; what is important is the people, and the ideas come second.

This is moving through adolescence, you see, at the age of half a century; it's one's early twenties.

Biles: You are talking actually about a technical matter, aren't you?

Golding: No, not really.

Biles: I mean the conveying of the idea through the vehicle of the believable person involved in the situation, which implies the idea, rather than the expounding of the idea as idea.

Golding: I'm not sure it is as simple as that, because I think it comes to who is the referee and who is the player? Is the idea the referee, who blows his whistle to stop the game at any moment, or is the person the referee, who can say, "Right, you thought you were playing soccer, but you really were playing something else"?

Biles: Shall we turn to the military, apropos of *Lord of the Flies?* What occurred during the war that changed your thinking, other than the evident fact that everyone grew up a bit in those days? If my information is correct, and it has been gathered haphazardly, you were involved in a number of actions. Weren't you at the sinking of the *Bismarck?*

Golding: Uh huh.

Biles: Then, there is the practically unpronounceable Dutch place, Walcheren Island.

Golding: Uh huh.

Biles: Were these incidents specifically involved in changing your views? You were in no occupation force. Your statement was that up to, say, September 1939 or thereafter, like everyone else you had heard the reports about horrible events in Germany and you were literally unable to believe them. Then, when the war was over, you did believe those things and had apparently decided that, as Huxley says, since society is a collection of individuals, what the individuals are is what society is. You plainly thought so, when you wrote *Lord of the Flies.* To repeat the question, what happened during the war that changed your mind?

Golding: I don't think I can answer that question, except in general terms and by putting it this way: in a way one saw during the war much more . . . what *happened.* All this has nothing to do, directly, with Nazis or anything; it has much more to do with *people.* One had one's nose rubbed in the human condition.

It is too easy a thing to say that before the war I believed one thing and after the war I believed another. It was not like that. I was gradually coming up against people and I was understanding a bit more what people were like; and, also gradually, learning that the things I hadn't really believed, that I had taken as propaganda, were, in fact, *done*. This kind of thing, for example: only about fifteen miles down there [near Bowerchalke], meeting some people who were working on the drops into France, the occupied territory; going there twice—meeting a man one time and the next time not meeting him, and being told that he was probably being tortured to death at that moment. This kind of thing one gradually began to *see*, and, at the end, I *fully* believed in [the fact of] Nazism; one couldn't do anything else. Finally, there were films of it, and there it was.

I had to equate that, on the one side, with what I knew about people, on the other side. Now it would be terribly flattering to me to make out that I suddenly saw how horrific people could be, as compared to the nice people I had known for the last five years [of the war, Golding's term of service], but it wasn't so. I had seen enough in the last five years to know that these people [the "nice people"] are capable of that, too; that really this was an extension of the human condition; that what the Nazis were doing, they were doing because certain capacities in them, certain deficiencies, certain anything you like in them, had been freed, and they were just people like us, in different circumstances.

So I saw that it was no good saying, "Well, fine. America, Britain, France, China, have all won. Against the dirty swine." Because I just didn't believe it. I saw that humanity had been fighting against itself in a kind of endless war. But what had been fighting and what had been doing all these things? On the whole, *only* on the whole—I wouldn't like this to be misunderstood, as I'm *sure* it would be—if you could take the people out of the concentration camps and make concentration-camp guards of them, the situation would not be altered materially. Can you see at all what I'm talking about?

It was a much more gradual process than the kind of snap things I have said about it because I wanted to say snap things; one's got to account for things somehow. One can say "before the war, after the war," but it was a long and slow process, it was growing up to adolescence.

Biles: I should like to be very clear. You do *not* mean that in your childhood you were "overprotected," as the psychologists say?

Golding: I don't know how far one can say "overprotection." All I would say is that, when I was a child, one of the most important things, for example, was the League of Nations, which was a Great Idea, in neon lighting, and this kind of thing was, in a sense, more important than anything else. Criminals and prisons and anything else you can talk about which deals with the seamy side of life were admitted to exist, but it was a dark thing down there; whereas the idea of the brotherhood of man, and all the rest of it, was somewhere up here, towards which everyone normally tended. You see, one didn't tend down there; one tended up here.

But when I was thrown, like millions of other people—and I don't want to exaggerate this—was thrown into contact with my "own brothers," I began to find them much more complicated—and much less self-aware, this is the important thing. I could listen to people talking about "bloody Nazis," people who I knew *were* Nazis. Do you see, they were in fact Nazis; only they didn't happen to live in the Nazi social system. Of course, I got round to the point where I said to myself, "There must be an explanation of why there is a Nazi system in one place and not in another, because even if they were held back only by certain social sanctions or social prohibitions, the social prohibitions were there." So this is a point, too.

The lesson was not entirely that. It was shock treatment in a way, and I perhaps took the lesson too much to heart. But I don't know how to express it, except to say that during the war—and this has nothing to do with shooting at people or even with being shot at—it was partly seeing how perilous life was, but also very much to do with what is sometimes called "rubbing shoulders with people," rubbing faces, rubbing every damn thing with people, whether in trenches or swinging in a hammock—not an awful lot of space.

Biles: You said regarding Nazi Germany, and you said it specifically, that you were not talking about Nazis *per se* but about *people*. The implication is that what for the moment we are calling "Nazism" could occur in Britain or in the United States, because the triggering device is people rather than nationals—Germans, Britishers, et cetera.

So far, that is clear, but then we come around to those "restrictions" you mentioned, restrictions which prevented English Nazism, excluding, naturally, a very minor splinter group. For that matter, we had an insignificant American Nazi party. How do you account for the nonnational character of the Nazi persuasion, then, when Germany was a Nazi *state?*

Golding: I'm not historian enough to be able to answer that question, and you must be a historian before you can answer it. If you are talking about the Nazis, you have to say that you've got the distinction between somebody's being the emperor of the Holy Roman Empire and his being the king of England. If he is the Holy Roman Emperor, he is not going to bother about his home country and you are going to have a fragmented society, because in days when you could have nothing but a one-man centralized rule—I'm talking about medieval times—you did, in fact, get a pile of small countries, each with its little king. Put it this way, that in Britain you've got the Heptarchy, the seven kingdoms—that was fourteen hundred years ago—but you've got God knows how many countries, how many kingdoms, in Germany up to about 1870.

This is the brute fact of history; so that, if this is the explanation—I think it *could* be—you had in Germany no capacity, no historical precedent, no historical custom, for regarding all the Germans together, as being inhabitants of one country. You don't have, as we have, a long tradition of whatever else you were, you were, on the whole, British. You might be poor British or rich British, but you wouldn't tend to think of yourselves as people against whom you could fight. All this is nonsense, because we *did* fight, but it is a question of degree.

There has been in this country for about a thousand years a gradually emerging social sense, so that a mob in Britain is not as bad as a mob in some places. It is bad, as all mobs must be, but this is inherited, it's something handed down. Now Germany has never had this, which helps you to understand the Nazis.

Then you have to take into account the other thing, which Marxism doesn't take into account, the fact of genius. Hitler was a genius. He was an evil genius, if you like, and he caught Germany just when everybody's sins were boiling over. Instead of being brave and forgiving at the Treaty of Versailles, we squeezed to the pip-squeak; so every German had in him an immense inferiority complex: "We have been beaten, smashed down; we have got to put this right." We would have felt the same, you would have felt the same, anybody would have felt the same. It is a kind of merciless train of history, except that it is not quite mechanistic, because the one thing that can't be postulated is that at the precise moment this kind of evil genius will arise.

It is one of those terrifying things that at the moment when Germany was right for it, like the breaking of a boil, you get this man emerging. Then, you get all the potentialities of man, all the beastly potentialities of man, given free rein, and there it was.

Even so, if you could have switched babies in the cradle—I won't talk about Britain, because we have talked about Britain, I will say America—if you had switched babies in the cradle at the right historical moment, by and large, Americans would have done what Germans did and vice versa. With one exception, of course: that you might have switched babies and Hitler might have been a saint rather than what he was. Then history would have been different.

If history is far more complicated than people think, it is not mechanistic. It does depend to quite an extent on personality, but it also depends on trends and historical inevitabilities. You see, it is a mixture of the two, and this is the situation I was stuck with. I wasn't good enough, wasn't clever enough, to put this over completely; all I could say at the time was, "Look, for God's sake, this could have been *us*."

Now there are ways in which it couldn't have been us, as

I've tried to explain to you, because history is so complex, but there is this overwhelming thing that we must be so careful about—you must be in America, we must be here, and God knows who else must be.

Biles: I have noticed in reading some of the essays you wrote for *Holiday* magazine, as well as in other periodical writing of yours, that I frequently find what appear to be almost incidental references to our time in phrases like "this frightening world," "a corrupt present," "our wickedness"; then I find such a phrase as "the days of innocence." As I recall, "the days of innocence" comes from that little essay ["Digging for Pictures"] about some excavation around here [in Wiltshire], where you were trying to get your digging done before a runway was paved over the site. But you seem almost *regularly* to refer to "this frightening world." You give me a phrase like "the days of innocence" in connection with the bones of the old woman, and in *The Inheritors* we had the days of innocence, at least with "the people." But the reiterated phrase is some variant of "this frightening world." Is one to make anything of this?

Golding: I think only in general terms that will probably be understood by everybody. I can't remember the essay very clearly, but I think "the days of innocence" must be meant as the kind of bogus history we get presented with in terms of black and white, when, although there may have been evil, it was concentrated in a number of people who were "baddies." There were "goodies" on the other side. And I think in that essay I deliberately shot that down, by discovering some evil that was buried in the earth—which I literally did, of course.

Biles: You concluded that it was very likely a murder.

Golding: Yes. It was, *very likely.*

Biles: Which is hardly congruent with the idea of innocence.

Golding: When I say "the days of innocence," this is said with a kind of—oh, what?—I won't say "tongue in my cheek," because what I was kidding myself with—you know, one must escape from evil.

Biles: Self-deception?

Golding: Self-deception. One must escape from evil, and archaeology is one of those quiet, passive ways of escaping into a time when, perhaps, evil doesn't really matter, because it's "baddies," you see. The lesson to me was the old woman: as a reminder, you know, that we haven't gotten the age of innocence. There never was one. As long as you have had Homo sapiens, you have had wickedness, because that's what he's about.

Biles: I wrote this one day in a burst of stupidity. Here's the statement: "You seem to be antirationalist-scientific-progressivist . . .

Golding: Incredible!

Biles: How about that? "At least in the H. G. Wellsian implication." Would it be fair to say that, in the oversimple, textbook statement of the case, you incline away from the optimistic eighteenth-century idea of Progress, with a capital P, and toward the equally fabulous conception of the decline from the Golden Age? Of course, you have pretty well done away with the Golden Age, by the introduction of the murdered old woman.

Golding: Yes, but I think I would like very much to know what anybody means by "progress." I don't think you can mention that word unless you take it in defined terms. Now, although I produced it myself, I'm going to bring out a textbook phrase—it has become one—and that is that *Lord of the Flies* was an attempt to trace the defects of society back to the defects of the individual. Surely, in that case, a Golden Age must, can emerge only when the individual conquers his defects, and this could be described as progress.

How far this is possible, I don't know. I think it may be possible. It is all so complicated, because the saint is so often wrong, so often limited, so often tied to a theology which he expresses in words which then alter their meanings. If one's talking in terms of progress which is tied to the progress of the individual, what sort of progress, in what terms, and with reference to which kind of idea? I just don't know about this; it's too complicated for me. I see, I think I can see, that the only kind of real progress is the progress of the individual towards some kind of—I would describe it as *ethical*—integration and his consequent effect upon people who are near him.

How far society can progress by this means I wouldn't know. I think it could progress perhaps a long way, because the one thing about really good people—I suppose I am talking about saints—is the fact that their effect is incalculable. One could do a tremendous statistical evaluation, one could say here we have a country like medieval France, of ten million people. One Joan of Arc alters the course of history for ten million people, and, therefore, America now needs twenty saints. But this isn't true. You could have a saint who affected [individual] people here, there, and the other place, all the way around the globe, but who had no social effect, as such. You can have a man like John Bunyan, who apparently affected the people in his back street, and he happened to write a book which affected the whole of the Western world.

One can sense the value of . . . I wouldn't even call them "good" people, I would call them "spiritual" people—a better word, I think. One can sense the value of spiritual people, without having any possibility of assessing the results of their value or of saying in statistical terms how valuable they are. That is why you can't see the future at all.

It comes back to Hitler, you see. I mean Germany would have been a mess anyway, but Hitler insured that it should be the boil that burst; similarly, a saint or a spiritual person can do a comparable thing. Of course, we may rapidly be moving towards the time when there aren't any more spiritual people; in which case, my opinion is we will simply sort of fade out then. "Where there is no vision, the people perish." I think that is literally true, literally true.

Biles: You remember Housman? The Terence poem, isn't it, "Terence, this is stupid stuff"? Housman says that there is much good in the world, but much more ill than good and, therefore, like a wise man, I would train for ill; doubtless hope for good, but assuredly train for ill. What you have been saying has to do with villains and saints, but these are the extremes. What about the great multitude in between? Are they "good guys" or "bad guys" fundamentally?

Golding: You tell me. They are what we are stuck with.

Biles: Yes, of course, they are. But the Bible and Machiavelli say that man is by nature wicked. Plato and Rousseau say that man is by nature good. Now most people, on an experience of you restricted probably to *Lord of the Flies*, would say, "Golding is with Machiavelli and the Bible in representing men to be by nature evil." Are you saying that? We have our saints and our villains, but taking the great unwashed three billion . . . ?

Golding: Unwashed three billion. I don't think you can say. I think all you can say about the great unwashed three billion—which was your phrase, I'll not call it mine—the great unwashed three billion are, on the whole, potential. According as their intelligence is more used or less used and more or less effective, they are about balanced between potentiality for good and potentiality for bad, whatever that means.

I wouldn't say that, either. I would say that there is a path they walk along, and it can be a great, wide, broad road, as it was for me as a boy. There were certain things that I couldn't possibly do, because my parents were such and such. I was protected. I was walking down a great, broad road. Most of us have this; on the whole, we have a road stretching to the horizon laid down for us by our social system.

It is only when the road gets very narrow and has drops on either side that you begin even to think in terms of whether men are bad or good. You see, it's whether they can do something dramatic or not. Most of us are potential murderers and most of us are potential surgeons, nurses, all these things; but our path leads us so straight a line that, unless we are brought up by nature to be surgeons because we have three generations of surgeons behind us, we don't become surgeons. Can you see at all what I mean?

Biles: Yes.

Golding: We don't even get opportunities to sin or virtueize in a great way. We are pretty well balanced between the two. It's this complicated social system again, because, on the whole, the fall off the straight and narrow tends to be a fall into something worse than one would be otherwise. So that society, taken whole, is a good thing. It enables us to use our bright side. When we fall off, we fall off into our dark side. Of course, we are talking in spatial metaphors, which always get everybody mucked up. But as a generalization, the change from order to disorder means that people show the Original Sin, if you like, in themselves. On the whole, the straight road through the ordered universe enables people more easily to show their original virtue. That is as far as I go.

Biles: But the little boys [in *Lord of the Flies*] still showed the black side.

Golding: But that's just what I'm saying. They had no ordered society.

Biles: They *had* one. They came from one. They brought the tradition of one with them. They tried to have one, and it fell away. Moreover, the reason in the book is that it fell away because of what they were, and what they were was two or three things: they were freed of restraints; they could, therefore, do what *pleased* them rather than what they *should do*, and so they goofed off instead of building shelters and keeping up the fire, which we would all do.

Golding: Well, I was going to ask, "Why have we got police forces?"

Biles: Self-evident.

Golding: This is what I was saying, that it is the ordered society which keeps us in this shape, this viable shape, this social shape, and which enables us to show our bright side. The bright side is there all right.

Biles: Yes.

Golding: Take away these sanctions, and we fall into the dark side. But you must remember this, that the sanctions, the shape of society, are also the product of the human being. Here is where it gets so damned difficult.

Biles: You are saying that, given the nature of man, there is also society, and it seems to me that you are saying society is what it is because of the people in it, because they made it what it is, but that it is also, at one and the same time, something else.

Golding: I'm not sure I follow you over that one. You're probably being far too clever for me. I think you probably are, you know, because society is what men are, right?

Biles: Right. But you said that society exercises an authority vested in it by the members and that it operates to a good end. That under the aegis and under the authority and under the restrictions of that very society which these men made, this society causes them to be better than they would otherwise be. So that makes it what it is and something else.

Golding: What it is and something else. Aren't we giving too narrow a definition for society? I have been talking about the Western world. There *are* head-hunters still. There was Nazi Germany. There was Stalin's Russia. I don't know anything about China, but I'm prepared to believe anything you tell me about it. There are societies in India which do this, that, and t'other, and in Africa, et cetera, et cetera. I suppose what we are getting round to, finally, is the hopeless admission, in the middle of the twentieth century, that there is a hierarchy of society. The hierarchy of society must be based ultimately on a hierarchy of people. One can say that it is only by desperate efforts in one or two fortunate, or perhaps unfortunate, places on the surface of the globe that the bright side of man has been enabled to emerge even as dimly as it has, and this must be because of the nature of the people who built that society. Which is against everything we are now taught, is it not?

Biles: Let us go back to specifics now. Here is Jack. Jack was apparently a good boy, in our black-and-white terms; at least, he was ostensibly so, because he had risen to be the head of the choir. Then, you put him on the island, and very quickly Jack becomes a sort of villain. Well, he was a part of society and was successful in the society in which he had been.

Golding: Ah, but you see the point: he was a *part* of society; on the island he is *all* of it.

Biles: Or he wants to be.

Golding: No, he *is* all of it. As head of the cathedral choir, he has over him a choirmaster, a precentor, a dean, and, ultimately, a bishop. And a lot of adults. Well, he can't be anything more than head of the choir. You take all that off and examine what being head of the choir means. In other words, what you are using to a good end in your choir, in your nice, safe Salisbury society, is in fact something which in itself is vicious, just as you give a cop with sadistic views a club and you give him laws to go by, and he will become a good member of society instead of a bad one. But remember, the society is the product of people.

Biles: What you are saying is that in Salisbury Jack can't be the bishop, but on the island he can. In Salisbury he wanted to be the bishop, but it was impossible; thus, he went along as the head of the choir. On the island he can be the bishop, and the readiest and easiest way that presents itself to him to be the bishop is the simple employment of brute force. The boys would not elect him chief, because they recognized his willingness to resort to violence and they were fearful of delivering themselves voluntarily to his domination. Nonetheless, he is the biggest and strongest boy, and no one dares stand in his way when he decides to throw off the forms and act upon his primitive superiority. This part of it is clear enough.

Most of the critics whom I have read have said in this regard that Jack is evil, that his innate self is evil. It came into my mind, when you were talking a minute ago, that Plato says something to the effect that no man consciously does evil and that when a man does an evil thing, it actually is the result of ignorance rather than of intention. What he is seeking is that which he considers a good, not an evil. The reason he mistakes is he fails adequately to assess the situation, so that, with his mind on the achievement of what to him is a good, he fails sufficiently to weigh the concomitant or possible evils consequent to his act. He doesn't make a balance between them; if he did, he would not then follow the course. Plato says something approximately like this, which would make Jack by nature good but ignorant.

Golding: I think it would be fact that Plato had been ignorant, because he ignores the fact of people's liking the crunch when you clout somebody over the head. I would start the other way round and say that you have people of Jack's nature, who are by nature evil, but who can be so integrated into a larger society that their evil is canalized in a good direction or, at least, in a possible direction, after all. Myself, I don't regard a hangman as a person of great ethical power; I suppose he could be, but he has never seemed to me to be this sort of person. In Nazi Germany, you remember, there was an anti-Plato, when they discovered a couple of pathological killers, they used them in the [concentration] camps. They said, "These men are too good to waste." They integrated them into their kind of society.

The shape of Nazi society was simply that you did have

this black genius at the top of it. I am quite sure, however, you can have someone other than the black genius at the top who can manage to integrate into society, God forgive us, even the hangman, doing a job which is filthier than cleaning out the drains, but which has to be done, in the circumstances.

And so the hangman *can* be integrated into society. I think I must be pretty dumb here, because this seems to me very much the problem over Jack. The problem of—well, isn't it the problem of delinquency? If you can give a boy a box of paints and if he does go along with the box of paints, instead of smashing shopwindows he will paint pictures. You have diverted him. He must *do* something. It could be that he would crack eggs or even play football, work it out of himself somehow, because he is integrated into a bigger scheme. You can integrate people into a black scheme the way Nazis did, if you can integrate them into an off-white scheme such as we have.

It is so long since I thought about the problem in these terms. I would have taken it really in much simpler terms, and I do know boys—or did know boys—so well that these things seemed to me so obvious, that you have the desire of boys for a perfectly straightforward legalistic job in society and that they bring to it their nature, whatever that nature is. Now write out rules for them, and they will abide by the rules, provided the rules give them, perhaps, authority. Their desire, their real wish, for authority is to dominate other people. If they can be got to do this legally, that is a triumph for everybody.

One further thing I would say is that I always suspect, have always perhaps instinctively feared, have always—*suspected* is the word—anyone who wants power. This is one of the reasons why politicians, no matter how good, are suspect to me. I can see how anyone can get himself into a powerful position and be one of these people on the broad road—you know, who is willing to go along just giving. I suppose there can be tremendous idealism and all this, that, and t'other thing, but I don't see it somehow. It seems to be the dilemma we are faced with that, on the whole, the politician is likely to be a Jack and, at best, a Ralph—never a Simon.

Biles: With regard to your political orientation, your political feelings, would you describe yourself as liberal, conservative, or heterodox?

Golding: Left of center, I think.

Biles: Slightly left of center? Or considerably left?

Golding: Bitterly left of center. I don't *like* being left of center, but I'm left of center. I *think* I am.

Biles: This is a liberal view?

Golding: No, I don't think so. I think this is more socialist than liberal.

Biles: Socialist?

Golding: Yes.

Biles: But not Marxist? Only socialist.

Golding: No, I'm not a Marxist.

Biles: No, of course not.

Golding: Well, don't say "Of course not" as though it were a dirty word.

Biles: No, but what I was thinking was that to most people Marxism represents an extreme, and I do not think that you would go to an extreme. When you say "left of center," you mean left, but not extreme left. Is that fair?

Golding: Yes. The socialist organization of the world will be damned awful, but it won't be as bad as the other things we could get. That's really about what it comes to.

Biles: At the moment I don't remember whether this is something you said to me or whether it is something I read, but in talking about what you called "furtive optimism" in H. G. Wells, you said, "That view *felt* that there was some kind of social perfectibility, which there *may be*, but I didn't see it at that time." I think you said this to me about a year ago in connection with *Lord of the Flies*. But you also said things like this: you were talking about how one knows what he thinks, then he goes through a period of knowing what he doesn't think. You came back to this phrase "social perfectibility, which there *may be*." You were suggesting then the view enunciated in *Lord of the Flies*, that social systems won't solve the problem, but now you're suggesting that you have shifted from that a little bit back in the other direction?

Golding: Partly back in the other direction. Also I am older, which perhaps gives me a less bitter view of the situation. I suppose it is something like this: I was writing *Lord of the Flies* because of my feeling that people had been looking at systems rather than at people. Now, I can see, or I think I can see, that that's perfectly true, but it's again a swing of the pendulum. Although it is true that a good system with bad men will turn into hell, it is equally true that a bad system with good men will be a good deal nearer what you want it to be than hell is. This is action and reaction. I think it probably is true that if in Los Angeles, for example, there had been integration and money poured into schools for everybody and so on and so forth, you might have still got bitterness and all the rest of it, but you wouldn't have had a blowup. This is the organization of society affecting the individual. So I *have* shifted from that point of view, simply because I have moved further away from Belsen and Hiroshima and all the rest of it.

Biles: It's still this kind of eclecticism. You want to take what seems best out of that end and out of this end.

Golding: You're making me sound a very feeble kind of liberal person.

Biles: No. I didn't mean any such thing.

Golding: I know you may not have meant it, but not only are you making me sound that way, I think I probably *do* sound that way.

Biles: I couldn't disagree more. I think that the soundest thing that anybody with just plain horse sense can do is say there is some merit on each side, because there are good-hearted and intelligent people on each side.

Golding: Yes, but the trouble about that, you see, is that in all social situations, something has to be done or *positively* not done. Right? When you see all round a question, or think you see all round a question, it is almost invariable that you do nothing, because of a kind of helplessness, a sort of almost autistic thing, a sort of feeling that it can't be me, I can't turn over this question, there's so *much* to be said on both sides. Perhaps we've bred ourselves to the point where people like me should be put down, shot.

[I dissented and laughed at this last suggestion, but Golding continued.]

No, seriously. Don't misunderstand me. I don't want to be shot. I don't want to be put down. But what place for people like me is there in the twentieth century, as we know it now? Because, you see, we don't *really* have any effect. What we do is, in many ways, indulge our own capacity for understanding, and this in itself can become a vicious thing. It might even be that there is more to be said for somebody who goes right out on a limb in one way or another than for somebody who sits solidly in the middle, feeling one ham rock this way and the other ham rock that way and it's here I sit.

Biles: I do not think that the crackpot, single-minded fellow who goes charging off in all directions at once gets anything done. At least, he is not likely to get anything good done.

Golding: Well, you know, you wouldn't have had the War of Independence if they'd all thought that way.

Biles: But, you see . . .

Golding: On the other hand, was that a terribly good thing? Now you tell me.

Biles: Well, now, with my Anglophilia, it's a little difficult . . .

Golding: You make it sound like a disease.

Biles: Well, it is a disease with me, rampant and incurable.

Golding: You'll get over it.

The Teller versus the Tale

In a BBC television interview for "Monitor," Golding spoke of the author's control of his material.

Interviewer: Don't you ever find meanings in the finished article you hadn't expected to find? Or intended?

Golding: No, I don't think so. I feel that what I meant at first is then written. I can imagine that a painter can entirely visualize a painting, and then just paint what he's visualizing. I think I write like that.

Interviewer: Do you think it's possible that a reader may understand your novels better than you yourself?

Golding: He can understand it in a different way, but I would guess that he can't understand it in a better way, because the—well, let's put it this way, that the one on the receiving end is the critic, and at the shooting end is the author. Now before the author shoots—when he is writing his book—he gets to know his book in a way no critic can possibly know it, even if he reads it twenty times.

I'm against the picture of the artist as the starry-eyed visionary not really in control or knowing what he does. I think I'd almost prefer the word "craftsman." He's like . . . one of the old-fashioned shipbuilders, who conceived the build of the boat in their mind and then, after that, touched every single piece that went into the boat. They were in complete control; they knew it inch by inch, and I think the novelist is very much like that.

In "The Meaning of It All," broadcast August 28, 1959, on the BBC Third Programme, Golding and Frank Kermode disagreed over the interpretation of the character Simon in Lord of the Flies.

Kermode: Yes, but may I introduce the famous Lawrence caveat here, "Never trust the teller, trust the tale"?
Golding: Oh, that's absolute nonsense. But *of course* the man who tells the tale if he has a tale worth telling will know exactly what he is about, and this business of the artist as a sort of starry-eyed inspired creature, dancing along, with his feet two or three feet above the surface of the earth, not really knowing what sort of prints he's leaving behind him, is nothing like the truth.

Golding pondered Kermode's acceptance of the Lawrentian dictum and reversed himself. In 1963, Faber and Faber published a school edition of The Brass Butterfly, *for which Golding provided a brief introduction. He postulates three uses for authorial introductions and advocates: "read the book first and be so interested that you turn back to the introduction to see what the author thought he was up to" (Emphasis supplied).*
So entirely has Golding changed his mind that he out-Lawrences Lawrence and semiseriously aligns himself with the Socratic attitude that almost no one speaks so ineptly of

poetry as the poets themselves. In "Fable," one of Golding's
lectures in America, he spoke of his change of mind: "For I
have shifted somewhat from the position I held when I wrote
the book [Lord of the Flies]. *I no longer believe that the*
author has a sort of patria potestas *over his brainchildren.*
Once they are printed they have reached their majority and
the author has no more authority over them, knows no more
about them, perhaps knows less about them than the critic
who comes fresh to them, and sees them not as the author
hoped they would be, but as what they are."

Golding: One of the terrifying things, if I may say so with
all diffidence, about the academic world is its consciousness.
Why can't it go along having a bit of unconsciousness?
Mrs. Golding: And its imputation of consciousness.
Golding: Its imputation of consciousness, yes. As though
books were really written for doctoral theses, you know.
Biles: Yes. Quite.
Golding: As far as I can see, to use another cliché, the
image that I project in the American academic world is of a
man brooding very much over the whole of his career, writing
in a rather Miltonic way: "Here lies old Hobson. Death
hath broke his girt," and all the rest of it, but knowing that,
ultimately, he's going to write *Paradise Lost,* you see. I think
this happens only once in the history of the world, perhaps.
In fact, what happens is you're a person who is trying to
live a normal life and who is wondering, in the name of God,
what else there is left to say, whether you've got anything to
say, whether what you said was any use anyway, and tearing
your clothes over the books you write. In fact—put it this
way—that what men write is the books they can, not the

books they should; so that when people talk about the meaning of a book, and all the rest of it, I can't answer that for myself. I could far more easily answer it for Angus [Wilson] or for Iris Murdoch than I can for myself, because, in fact, if there *is* a meaning to the books, then it's gone by the time you've written the book; otherwise, there wouldn't be any point in writing the book, in a sense. The book must be some kind of deed at some particular moment, and the man who writes the book is surely the last possible person to be able to tell you anything about it. Can you see at all what I'm getting at? It's really rather like expecting a mother to be a gynecologist.

Biles: You wrote the book, and there the book is; now, it is the critic's business, I guess, to haggle about the book. The book, there it is.

Golding: What I just said may sound very unkind or ungracious, but it isn't really like that at all, because obviously I'm immensely flattered by people's asking me questions, and I'd be a fool if I didn't say so. Equally I'd be a fool if I thought I could answer them.

Biles: But look at it this way: you have already answered them, before the fact; what I mean is that the book is the answer.

Golding: Well, is it? I don't know. I'm not sure whether it answers, or anything. When we were talking about society—about the bright side of man and the dark side, and the wide road and the cliffs, and all the rest of it—I knew there was something there that one should say, but really, finally, all one is left with is the kind of infinite complication of any given situation. And, therefore, one is also left with the infinite complication of the answer to any question, because any book is infinitely complicated, no matter how simple it looks. That's about what it comes to. God knows how people can write theses; I couldn't.

Biles: The other day I got the ground cut from under my feet, which always happens. I had my sleeves all rolled up and I had come over to have a real head-butting session with you about a thing you said to Frank Kermode.

Golding: What was that?

Mrs. Golding: I could see your smile just now, Jack, and I guessed you were remembering that.

Biles: Last Monday, I went up to Manchester to see Frank and somehow the D. H. Lawrence warning against tale-tellers came up in passing. Frank said, "Do you know one of the most interesting things? I had a letter from Bill Golding, and he has changed his mind." Tell me one thing: why did you change your mind? Do you know?

Mrs. Golding: Because he got asked so many questions.

Golding: As a matter of fact, Frank was sitting right where you are now, and the BBC stuck a microphone in through that window and had a truck on the lawn there, and we sat and argued this out, and I said these things, you see. Now, this is the real truth of the matter, that it was an argument, a very friendly argument, but one couldn't possibly agree with Frank. It was such a friendly argument that one had to disagree. I thought I knew what I meant when I wrote the book [*Lord of the Flies*], and Frank brought this up, and I said, "Oh, nonsense."

Biles: Your phrase was *"absolute nonsense."*

Golding: Yes, one of those "friendly remarks." But, of course, as in all really good conversations, what happened— the best thing that happened—was afterwards, when I went away and thought about what he had been talking about. I thought, "Maybe he's got something there." As time went on, I began to agree more and more, and now, I think, if he were sitting where you are, probably the conversation would be reversed. He would be saying, "Oh, come, you know far more about the books than that." This is really what happened.

As far as I was concerned, it was an educational jaunt. It really was. Frank taught me something; he brought to my notice, in a big way, something which I hadn't really thought about before.

Mrs. Golding: I think time has helped to teach you this, too, in that people have found so many different things in your books.

Golding: This is perfectly true, that one gets contrasting interpretations. Now I have a kind of standard remark that I make for students when they write me letters. I write back and I say, "What is in a book is not what the author thought he put in, but what the reader gets out of it; so your guess is as good as mine." That is really what I tell them, and I think it is true.

The Business of Writing

Biles: How do you write, easily or laboriously?

Golding: Well, I have never been able to answer, honestly or not. It is . . . Oh, Ann, how do I write?

Mrs. Golding: Well, sometimes you write very easily. I mean that you write very quickly, when you are writing. Oh, when you are involved with something and you are extremely interested in it, it comes quickly. I don't mean to say it is the final draft the first time.

Biles: No, of course not.

Mrs. Golding: That is true, isn't it?

Golding: Yes.

Mrs. Golding: And you can write the draft of a novel in three weeks. You have done it.

Golding: Yes. Yes, *The Inheritors* got written in three weeks. But the trouble is, you see, I then get stuck with nothing to say to anyone for a long, long time. This enables me to learn to play the piano, but it doesn't do much else.

Biles: But you are talking now about gestation, aren't you? You think about the book, you plan the book, and when the time comes, the book comes, and you write it with facility and with rapidity. Is that approximately correct?

Golding: If you will forgive my saying so, this is a rather

Piggy-like view of the thing, because it sounds like adding one to another and there it all goes. What happens really is that I go on for a long time firmly in the belief that I'm never going to write another word. *Literally,* this is. You know, I can't think how anybody *can* write another word, and I reason with myself and say, "Nonsense. Of course it will happen again." And it doesn't, and I get very depressed.

Mrs. Golding: I think this could be completely overplayed, because I don't think you get as desperate as I am told some people do.

Golding: Well, now, I don't.

Mrs. Golding: You know you don't really say to yourself, "I'm never going to write again," so much as you say to yourself, "That is the sort of thing that people might be saying to themselves if they found themselves in my position."

Golding: Yes, that's it. It's perfectly true. It's very inside out and wheels within wheels, but it does feel like that very much. And then, quite suddenly, "Bang!" Do you see?

For example, *Lord of the Flies.* I was sitting one side of the fire and Ann was sitting the other, and I had just been reading a God-awful book to—not to you, Judy [the Goldings' daughter], because you were too young for this at the time—to David [the Goldings' son], a book about boys on an island, the usual adventure story. It wasn't *The Coral Island* [1857, by Robert Michael Ballantyne (1825–1894)] or anything else. I remember saying to Ann, "Oh, I'm so tired of this business. Wouldn't it be fun to write a book about boys on an island and see what really happens?" And she said, "That's an awfully good idea. You do that." So I got a piece of paper and started to work out the story, and then everything went on, just like that, and there was no strain beforehand.

===

*On "working out the story," Golding replied to an inter-
viewer's question about his method, "I plan a novel from the
beginning out to the end, before I write anything. In detail.
I see it in the air as a kind of bulbous shape about so long,
from here to here [gesturing with hands held apart], and then
the detail begins to fill in, and I work it out until almost the
last flick of an eyelid. And then I write through from one
point to the other."*

Golding: Before *The Inheritors*, I had an awful lot of
strain, because I was trying to write three other books, none
of which I ever did write and none of which was any good.
Then I thought—I got desperate—I thought I *must* write a
book; so I more or less sat down and wrote *The Inheritors* in
three weeks. And so on, like this.

There is no gradual evolution, no sense that, now I've
reached my age, I ought to be writing *my* book, you know. I
don't know what *my* book is or who *I* am or where *we* are or
anything else; so I don't know what I should write about.

Mrs. Golding: The gestation could be rather like this. It
could be a sort of covert pregnancy.

Golding. "Trunk of humors."

Biles: With *The Inheritors* you obviously had seized upon
—or had been seized upon—because you wrote the book in
three or four weeks. That means hard at it and lickety-split,
during the time. How long did *Lord of the Flies* take?

Mrs. Golding: From the first draft to the last was about
three months, four months, wouldn't you think?

Golding: Something like that.

Biles: Three or four months for *Lord of the Flies.*

Golding: This was several drafts.

Biles: Are you saying, then, that there were not several drafts of *The Inheritors,* that you wrote it and revised it and that was all?

Golding: There were two drafts. There was one draft of *The Inheritors* which I wrote in three weeks. The second one I think I typed. I believe this is right. I didn't write a second draft in longhand. I wrote the first one in longhand at about—oh, between two and three thousand words a day, something like that, in three weeks, three weeks plus. Then, I decided what was wrong with it and did the next draft on a typewriter, and, substantially, that was the one that was published. I think I made three or four alterations in it, perhaps half a page at a time.

Biles: Fascinating. Here we get *Lord of the Flies* in three or four months and *The Inheritors* in one month. What about *Pincher Martin?*

Golding: I can't remember about *Pincher,* except that it was done on the typewriter.

Biles: You ordinarily write with a pencil?

Golding: I don't know which I do. I have just written [December 1964] a twenty-five-thousand-word-long short, which I wrote with a pen ["Inside a Pyramid," *Esquire,* December 1966], but *The Spire* I did all on typing. It depends very much on what goes on. There is no rationality about it.

Biles: One can't tell from the outside, of course, but I would have supposed that a good deal more time went into the writing of *Pincher Martin* and *Free Fall* and *The Spire* than went into these first two. I knew that *The Inheritors* had been written in a very brief time; I did not know that *Lord of the Flies* was written so quickly. Is that more or less correct?

Golding: I think it is true of *Pincher Martin.* It may be true of the last two, I wouldn't know. I think *Pincher Martin* was written pretty quickly, very much so.

Mrs. Golding: In fact, you wrote most of it—that's the first draft—in one Christmas holiday, on vacation from the end of term to the beginning of the next term.

Biles: This is, again, a matter of two or three weeks?

Mrs. Golding: A matter of four weeks.

Biles: Four weeks.

Mrs. Golding: But it's a draft.

Biles: Yes, of course.

Mrs. Golding: Do you remember, Bill, you did quite a bit at Marlborough?

Golding: I remember that. By Jove, I wish we had had to do this about Shakespeare [instead of about Golding].

Biles: Envoy Extraordinary and "Miss Pulkinhorn" I suppose you wrote very quickly, since each is short?

Golding: Yes.

Biles: What of *Free Fall* and *The Spire?* What lengths of time were devoted to composition of these, would you say?

Golding: Well, a great deal more time. I can't remember *Free Fall* much. I think that was longer than the first three.

Biles: Yes, it is longer.

Golding: Yes, but I wasn't thinking of that. I believe that it took longer to write, not in the sense that the same things got rewritten. It changed a lot. I can't remember how it changed, but it did. It was reorganized, and things were thrown out and things put in.

Biles: Not customary Golding practice, is it?

Golding: To this extent, no. In *The Spire* . . . I have forgotten when I was in America—two years ago?—at Hollins . . . or three? Something like that.

Biles: Academic year 1961–1962.

Golding: Well, in '61, when I was in England, I played about a bit with a draft of that; then I went to America. While I was at Hollins, I wrote a draft of it which took me about . . . what? . . . three? . . . two? . . . weeks, I think. Then I came home and started to work on it again, and dropped it, and took it up. So you see, this had gone on a long time; this is several years, in a way. The point is I hadn't been working at it for more than one burst and then another burst. The last draft, like the first one, was written in perhaps a month, that sort of time.

Biles: I was curious, for, among other reasons, there are five years between *Free Fall* and *The Spire.*

Golding: As much as that, is it?

Biles: The Spire is 1964 and *Free Fall* is 1959.

Clarity and Technique

A BBC *television interviewer for "Monitor" talked with Golding shortly after the publication of* Free Fall. *He quoted Sammy Mountjoy, "Art is partly communication, but only partly. The rest is discovery." Then he asked, "Do you see yourself as a communicator or a discoverer?" Golding replied: "Well, I'm living. Tomorrow I shall be a little different, as yesterday I was a little different. My views change, as long as I'm alive and aware. I just can't tell you what the balance is in any particular situation. It varies between the two. At one moment one may be wanting to communicate more than to discover, and at another one may be making the effort to discover, and communication fades into the background. But I—this may seem strange to you—I do think that art that doesn't communicate is useless. Mind you, you may create it, but it remains useless if it doesn't communicate."*

Biles: There is at least a possible divisibility of opinion concerning the proposition that the artist, if he has something to say which is or may be to the benefit of mankind, is or should be under some moral obligation to be as communicative, as clear, as he can be. Or, conversely, that the artist does not have the right, which T. S. Eliot assumed in *The*

Waste Land and elsewhere, to demand of the reader that the reader learn a special vocabulary or acquire esoteric knowledge in order to grasp what it is he has to say. What is your feeling about the moral obligation of the artist and the question of clarity?

Golding: I think one of the things that's the matter with us, surely at the moment [January 3, 1965], is that almost anything that is not worth saying can be said with infinite clarity and anything which is worth saying can only be put across in a special kind of thought-way which hits people at many levels and says to them, "Now look here, this is not a Coca-Cola advertisement, this is not a pronouncement by the Senate or the President or the Queen or whatever, this is a particularly relevant set of communications being made to whoever can grasp it."

I'm not really being clear in this. I suppose what I am saying is that it's no good being clear, because to be clear is to be unnoticed. Anyone can say, "Don't drink and drive. You must drink coffee." But then this doesn't begin to touch the reason why people drink and drive. You know that the only way you can really get hold of somebody who drinks and drives is not by talking about drinking and driving, but by putting him in a position where he understands some kind of process—it may be emotionally understanding, not intellectually understanding.

Biles: Do you think, if the artist has something to say for the benefit of mankind, that he is under some obligation to say it as lucidly as he can, however complex the statement might be, or do you think it legitimate for him to say, "You can simply learn my language"?

Golding: I don't think he can say that because, to begin

with, nobody is going to learn the language unless he wants to. *If* the complexity of his language is a result of what he is saying, *if* people are willing to learn that language, then he is successful; whereas, if he just becomes complex trying to explain complexity and nobody gives a damn, well, then he's no good.

It's all these things. One can't analyze them down to the last inch; there is so much a question of "feeling" and "as it goes at this moment." Take a straightforward example: when you are telling a story, one of the technical things is not to tell a bit of it, because if you wait for a chapter and then your reader thinks, "My God, that's what happened! He never said so, but that's what happened," this is ten times more powerful a communication than the direct saying of "Then he went and then he did."

This is a question of technique, which is the responsibility of the writer, because he is trying to say something, trying to affect somebody, and if he does it this way, then it is the responsibility of his position to say, "I *must* fool him this long, because at the end of it I'm going to hit him for six; you see, I'm really going to hit him hard there." Because he needs to be hit hard there.

That is why this question of complexity and clarity is so mixed up. It is really in the hands of the writer. Doubtless, I suppose, you have to give an ambassador a mandate and say, "You may say, within limits, this much, because you are doing an important job." The writer has to say, "I am trying to say something important, and if I have to fool this man in order to hit him in the belly at the right moment, I will do this. If he is angry with me because I didn't just *say*, it's because it's none of his business." He is not a writer, you see; he is just a reader. A reader is somebody who is magical, or ought to be magical. Does that make any sense?

Biles: These are exactly the kinds of things I would say about the comprehensive, extending irony at the ends of your books, what Gindin insists is a "gimmick" [originally, as applied to his books, Golding's term]. To maintain stubbornly that the final twists are only gimmicks seems to me to miss the point precisely in connection with what you have been saying. The only case in which most people whom I have talked to tend to side with the gimmickry attitude is the twist at the end of *Pincher Martin.*

Golding: Yes.

Pincher Martin

One example of a moderate statement of dissatisfaction with the "gimmick" ending of Pincher Martin—*and there are immoderate objections, like those of James Gindin—is the remark made by Angus Wilson:* "Even in Pincher Martin, *my own doubt is how much the pay-off at the end really strengthens the novel, whether this doesn't belong more to a short story than to a novel, if you know what I mean. The thing* [Pincher Martin] *is so great, so considerable on its own account, that when you get to that end, you say, 'Ah, yes, I see,' and you think, 'How clever, how wonderful,' but then you think afterwards, 'Yes, but did it really add to all that I had known already?'* "

Biles: I specially wanted to hear you on this, because of *Pincher Martin.* Though I doubt it, it may be that there is more substance to the objection to the ending of *Pincher Martin* than to the endings of the other books. What do you think about it?

Golding: Well, I don't know, really. I suppose it is possible, because *Pincher Martin* is a book in which, once you start with a basic premise, there is really nothing which is irrelevant, and the difficulty becomes one of choice—or of one's selection, if you want—not one of discovery.

It may have been a mistake on my part, but the mistake on my part was really one stemming from a miscalculation of the amount of straightforward theological knowledge which is still washing round with people. I thought people would have a natural interest in theology, which, on the whole nowadays, they haven't. Therefore, it seemed to me that when early on in the book this man—the other man, I have forgotten his name now—talked about heaven . . .

Biles: Nathaniel.

Golding: Nathaniel. He said that heaven would be like a black lightning, meaning you [Pincher Martin] couldn't appreciate it, you've got nothing in common with it, and therefore it would be just sheer destruction. I thought this was the key of the book and people would see it. If they didn't, I thought when they got round to the sea boots [at the end], then it would be perfectly obvious that Pincher's was a purgatorial experience. But no. I think it was a miscalculation on my part of the degree to which people were going to go along with me on this one, of the degree to which they would take it as a straight adventure story.

Biles: If you could change the book now, would you simply cut the last sentence? Somebody—maybe it was V. S. Pritchett [actually, Hilary Corke, in *Encounter*, February 1957]— recommended the excision of the last line, in which the statement is made that Pincher *did* drown right off, but you wouldn't change that?

Golding: Well, you see, that is asking me to take something that was stood on its head and put it the right way up again. The whole point of the book is that it was stood on its head. Pritchett is, I suppose, a straightforward twentieth-century humanist, and this is not what I am, I don't think, and this isn't what the book is about. No, I wouldn't change the ending.

Biles: A 1956 reviewer of *Pincher Martin* for *The New Statesman and Nation* said that *Pincher Martin* is "a misleading title for readers of W. W. Jacobs." This was a trifle confusing.

Mrs. Golding: There is another book called *Pincher Martin.*

Golding: The book is about an ordinary seaman. I think it is a First World War book called *Pincher Martin, O.D.* [ordinary deckhand]. It is a funny book about amusing adventures that happened to an ordinary seaman. Now I am not quite sure, historically speaking, about which way round it is, but certainly Martins are called "Pincher" in the Royal Navy. I don't know whether they are called "Pincher" because of this book or whether they were already called "Pincher" and the author appropriated the name. I am relatively sure that "Taffrail" wrote *Pincher Martin, O.D.*

Biles: I looked into a catalogue of books in print at Dillon's the other day, and four or five books by "Taffrail" were listed, but there was none called *Pincher Martin, O.D.* Naturally, this does not mean there was no such book, only that it is not in print.

Golding: I am quite sure the book exists, and I do believe I have read it. I am sure I must have read it sometime. Indeed, I am confirmed in that, because when I wanted to call mine *Pincher Martin,* it was okay, but about six months later I met Charles Monteith [Golding's editor at Faber and Faber], whom you met, and he was talking to another man. It came out that they had to go to the British Museum Library to check up on this title, and they found it was one I could use, because the other book had been called *Pincher Martin, O.D.*, so my title was okay. That one does exist, and I do remember reading it, but all I can remember is that it is a series of stories about a rather frivolous naval person.

Pincher Martin and Free Will

Biles: I can't seem to get finally straight about whether we are talking about Rockall in *Pincher Martin.* [Rockall is a tiny point of rock seventy feet high located approximately 184 miles nearly due west of St. Kilda, the remotest of the Hebrides, at latitude 57° 36′ 20″ north, longitude 13° 41′ 32″ west.] I say we are.

Golding: Well, we are. But, of course, it doesn't exist [for Martin], so are we?

Biles: We are talking about that tooth, too, of course.

Golding: We are talking about the tooth, too, but Rockall is the only sensible rock that Pincher could possibly find himself on, because he is in the North Atlantic.

Biles: I read a book about Rockall.

Golding: Did you? Ah, yes, James Fisher!

Biles: Yes.

Golding: Good old James! He and I have a tidy club. You know, we both belong to it.

Biles: Well!

Golding: The Rockall Club. He's been on it, and I've written a book about it.

Biles: It is simply that people say "yea" and "nay" about Rockall.

Golding: It is irrelevant, isn't it? You see, Pincher is not there; he's not anywhere.

Biles: Yes, I understand that. But the thing is that I was persuaded, particularly after reading Fisher's book, that there is no question but that Rockall is the source for the description, the relationship to the tooth.

Golding: Pincher does say [of Rockall], as a kind of flashback, to the navigating officer, the captain, "I'd call it a near miss," meaning "fuck all," which is very nearly what "Rockall" is. It looks like that [gesturing]. Just that, in the middle of two, three thousand miles of water.

Biles: In *Pincher Martin,* do you mean by the "unexamined centre" that thing within the body which *is* the man; whether one calls it "personality" or "the spirit" or whatever; it is that which is gone when the man is dead?

Golding: Well, I think you're jumping the gun a bit with the second half of that one, because I don't know about that. I would say it is a simple, almost arithmetical, proposition. You think about yourself, and no matter how many layers you strip off, there is always something thinking about yourself. The thing which is thinking, which is examining, cannot examine itself, you see, because it is the thing which is examining. It's like the telescope, which can't examine itself; the eye can't see itself without a mirror, because it is actually doing the job. There is deep inside any man just this one point of awareness which cannot examine itself, because it is working when it tries to examine.

Biles: To put it in these terms, you mean that it is a mechanical impossibility; you don't mean there is some sort of metaphysical restriction that prevents the thing from looking at itself? It is a *mechanical* impossibility.

Golding: Well, a *factual* impossibility. I don't know whether that is mechanical or metaphysical.

Biles: But, as you say, the eye cannot look at itself. There are no necessary overtones to be drawn from this; it just can't be done.

Golding: It is the defeat of the amateur theologian, if you like, or of the amateur metaphysician; this is where he passes out.

Biles: I don't know what existentialism is, do you?

Golding: Does anybody?

Biles: Some people—I suppose largely on *Pincher Martin* —find you existential. The existentialists seem to be concerned with the matter of identity, but they take a view that you don't take. They take the view that man is absurd, that his position in the universe is absurd. You certainly don't take that view. But because of *Pincher Martin* and the identity business . . . I suppose that's why people suggest that there is an existential element in your books.

Golding: Well, you see, I can only answer one way, which is going to sound a bit lofty. People have done a sort of Freudian exegesis on me. Well, I don't know my Freud, but both Freud and I have been looking at ourselves and human society. There must be points at which we agree. Well, now, my generation is the existentialist generation.

Biles: John Peter quotes a letter from you about the cellar in *Pincher Martin,* and he quotes you as saying "God is the thing we turn away from into life, and therefore we hate and fear him and make a darkness there." Would you elaborate that just a little bit?

Golding: Well, I suppose it was an attempt to rationalize theology or to rationalize a theological concept, which is always a dicey thing to do. But it was founded at bottom on the proposition that man has free will and that man was created in God's image and had free will because he was created in God's image, that he had free will the way God has it. Well, once you have free will and you are created, you have alternatives before you. You can either turn towards God or away from Him. And God can't stop you turning away from Him without removing your free will, because that's what free will is. This is the whole thing about *Pincher Martin*. It's that and nothing else. When you turn away from God, He becomes a darkness; when you turn towards Him, He becomes a light, in cliché terms. But I think that's about it.

Biles: This more or less squares with Milton's view, doesn't it?

Golding: Does it?

Biles: Doesn't it? I mean, in *Paradise Lost,* the freedom of the will and the rest.

Golding: "Free to fall," yes.

Biles: "Sufficient to have stood, though free to fall"—that's the heart of the matter. And the turning away. The reason God seems dreadful to Pincher Martin is really that Martin has returned the favor; he has created God in Pincher Martin's image. Pincher Martin is hateful; therefore God appears to him as hateful.

Golding: Well, God can only play with him on his own terms.

Biles: Right. Otherwise, freedom of the will goes down the drain.

Golding: Well, the thing is really this: if you give Pincher free will, there is only one way in which you can get Pincher out of hell, that's by destroying him, because if you take his free will away, he's no longer Pincher. He's no longer made in God's image. So God is stuck with a paradox which He can resolve, presumably; I can't. But what happens to somebody who exercises his free will and goes on exercising it? What's to be done?

Free Fall or Free Will

Biles: Of all your books, the one which has been least praised—indeed, even panned—in the press has been *Free Fall.* A matter that the critics have always chewed on, one thing that turns up over and over and over, is that in your books you tend to isolate your characters, that you don't provide the broad social panorama that is the traditional stuff of the novel. Well, in *Free Fall* you have come closer to what they've been yelling for, but they still aren't satisfied.

Mrs. Golding: I remember other people have said that they find there is more to be got personally from *Free Fall*—particularly younger people—that it speaks to them more directly in some way.

Golding: Um.

Biles: We ought to be fair. Although there have been people who have been rather down on *Free Fall,* there have been many others who have praised it highly. Bill, would you agree that the idea is sound that *Free Fall* may be considered a fiction—a philosophic and symbolic fiction, but still a fiction—a book of a different sort altogether from the others? You recall the differentiation of fiction, fable, and myth which you and Frank Kermode discussed.

Golding: Probably an attempt to write a different sort of

book. How far it's successful I don't know. I suppose in a sense it is an attempt to put the story, in so far as it is a story, within circumstances that are recognizable to most people of my own generation. Just *that*. You know, most of us haven't been on an island in the middle of the Pacific or in the middle of the Atlantic or been closely to do with Neanderthal man, and I thought it was perhaps time I had electric light in the streets and all that. No more than that. . . .

Well, now I'm going to sound pretentious, probably. I think I have probably sounded pretentious already, but I do want to try and put this over—because it is important to me —that, as experience, it seems to me that we do live in two worlds. There is this physical one, which is coherent, and there is a spiritual one. To the average man—with his flashes of religious experience, if you like to call them that—that world is very often incoherent. But nevertheless, as a matter of experience, for *me* and I suspect for millions of other people, this experience of having two worlds to live in all the time—or not all the time, [but] occasionally—is a vital one and is what living is like. And that is why this book is important to me, because I've tried to put those two worlds into it, as a matter of daily experience. . . .

Free Fall was an invention from beginning to end, a deliberate invention. All the terms of my life were turned upside down. My boyhood and most of my life—I might say *all* of my life—have been hideously respectable. But I was concerned very much with the question of freedom of action, and I finally found I couldn't explain this in any way. But I set these things up: for example, I said to myself, "You were in the navy; well, this man has to be in the army. You are a writer; you'll have to make this man a painter." And so, all the way round, the whole thing was an invention in much the same way that *Envoy Extraordinary* was an invention. Even so far as the question of "What was there that happened to people during the war?" which brought the whole question of freedom of action up in the most poignant way. And of course the thing that immediately comes to mind, I suppose, is, in fact, to be a prisoner, and so I did this, too.

Biles: If I understand, you are saying that you followed substantially the method that you followed in those earlier books: you took something and stood it on its head; you took your respectable schoolmaster's-home kind of background and postulated that the son was a slum child.

Golding: Yes, yes.

Biles: I am pleased to hear you say so, because it has always seemed evident to me that *Free Fall* is to a considerable degree autobiographical, in such an inverted way.

Golding: I see, yes.

Biles: Some days ago I saw a television interview with you, from the time when *Free Fall* was newly published.

Golding: With me? Television?

Biles: This was a BBC thing called "Monitor." I am very much interested to see what you say, because you are subjected to the same questions over and over. It is very informative to see what you say in answer to these questions at different times, since it is not always exactly the same.

Golding: Obviously not.

Biles: Obviously not, since you don't have a set of Teutonic prearranged answers which you give. One of your remarks in the BBC interview hit me hard. You told the young BBC interviewer, *"Free Fall* is important to me," and I wondered what you meant by this, whether you meant merely that *Free Fall* is important to you in the way that all of a man's books are naturally important to him or whether you meant that this book has some sort of special importance. Do you have any idea what you meant then? What do you mean, now?

Golding: I honestly don't know what I meant, except the question of freedom. All it really boils down to is, I suppose, the endeavor that every man has—and some succeed more than others—to make one of these Teutonic forms, to be a Lutheran, to be a Catholic, to be a Buddhist, or to be something.

The particular poignancy, as I see it, of what I may call the model intellectual of the twentieth century—which is what we most of us are, unless we have committed ourselves to something; in which case, we're lucky—the poignancy of the model intellectual is that he is literally in this state of free fall.

Everybody has translated this in terms of theology; well, okay, you can do it that way, which is why it's not a bad title, but it is in fact a scientific term. It is where your gravity has *gone;* it is a man in a space ship who has no gravity; things don't fall or lift, they float about; he is completely divorced from the other idea of a thing up *there* and centered on *there* in which he lives.

Do you see what I mean? Where for hundreds of thousands of years men have known where they were, now they don't know where they are any longer. This is the point of *Free Fall.* Perhaps I didn't mention this aspect at all in those days, possibly because I felt a little tiny bit ashamed of the kind of science-fiction overtones of *Free Fall,* but it is really and truly the idea. There is also the Miltonic idea; there is also the Genesis idea; there is also the ordinary daily life idea of something which is "for free," and something which is also "fall." "Free" and "fall" are both caught up in it.

Biles: Seeing this is why I got so excited when I reread it the other day.

Golding: The end of it, as I remember, is an attempt to put the other version, the two contrasting views of life, neither of which really makes sense because the other exists. Either, on its own, makes sense, but when you've got them both there—and this *is* the situation—neither one taken alone does.

Religion, Rationalism, and Morality

Biles: You used the expression that you are a religious man, but possibly an incompetently religious man. I have puzzled for a long time about why you used the word "incompetently."

Golding: I suppose that anyone who has any kind of religious leanings or finds himself falling flat on his face over a kind of trip wire with religion must come to the conclusion that he is not fitted for the situation he finds himself in.

Biles: Angus Wilson told me that your father had *no* religious beliefs; that is, he was a scientific rationalist of his time. Now *you* are a religious man.

Golding: Yes. When Angus says that, I think he is right up to a point, as indeed he would be. But it's a partial statement in this sense: that my father's absence of religious belief was really founded in a profound religious *feeling.* There are so many people who can go along with a sect they may be born into or a religion they may be born into, because it never troubles them. They wear it like an old coat. Not for my father. He was always questioning.

The reason why he had no religious beliefs was that he couldn't. He was brought up short every five minutes. I don't know what one would call this; he had an inarticulate poet's eye. Can you see what I mean through that statement? He was always stunned by the fact of things, do you see, and so, although he *said* he was a rationalist, I think, nevertheless, this was in many ways a matter of profound regret for him. He wasn't a man who scoffed at God. He was a man who regretted God so profoundly that he almost believed in Him. Like saying "There is no God, I've told Him so."

I'm standing on my father's shoulders here. I don't think that I believe myself to be wiser than my father. It's merely that he lived a long life, which I haven't lived. But then, on the other hand, I had the benefit of being his son, you see, of being brought up in this curious situation, where one really belonged to nothing.

Biles: But that sense of order which he had seems to me a religious matter. The idea of an order in the universe—well, really, in a way, that is what God is, or it is an aspect of God.

Golding: Well, I don't know about that. This may go all right for you, and it may be true, but as far as my father was concerned, all I can say is that I always had the feeling with him that if he had been born round the corner or on the other side of the street or in a different village or even perhaps five minutes earlier or later he would have been a preacher, you see, and most unpopular in any religion he was in.

Biles: It all redounds very much to his credit. You are saying very admirable things about him.

Golding: He was a man, all right. There is no question of that. But, anyway, the point was that he did have a profoundly—instinctively almost, one might call it, but I suppose it was merely habitual and not instinctive—we'll call it habitual moral view of life. This is the odd thing: he ended up with a kind of system, as I firmly believe that rationalists and many others do, a system in which there was no place, logically, for right and wrong. But all the same, right and wrong were there. Do you see, he was a profoundly moral man. I said to him very often, "What you say you believe in leaves no room for right and wrong. Why are you as moral as you are? Why do you believe in justice? And fair play, and all the rest of it?" He never saw this. It was a curious kind of blankness his generation had, and it goes right back to the middle of the nineteenth century at least. They never saw that the morals by which they lived were not deducible from the system which they held to apply. This is a most extraordinary thing, in the way that even Marxism is founded basically on Christian morality. This always was the thing, and there again, you see, in a way, *Free Fall* is only a kind of footnote to that situation, is it not?

Biles: You are a religious man. This is, in a sense, like your father. You are not formalized. You don't go through the social rituals of religion, do you?

Golding: No indeed, I don't. But this is not, I think, because of any stand I take. It's a difficult thing to describe. It's not laziness; but on the other hand, laziness has a part in it. In other words, I sound very much like a man who is looking breathlessly around the universe for something to do. This is not true. But, as I can't subscribe to any religion, so I don't make the appropriate gestures. I think probably, if I could subscribe to any religion, I should still find it very difficult to make the gestures. I'm a disorganized man, in that sense.

Biles: There is one man who has written several essays

proving to his satisfaction that you are a Calvinist. That strikes me as a bit rigid for you.

Golding: It might not be rigid for what I've written. I don't know whether I've ever said this to you, but it's something that I'm rather proud of, because I think it's a discovery of mine. That is, that men don't write the books they should, they write the books they can. Now I don't think it's true I'm a Calvinist, but I'm willing to believe that my capacity for writing, such as it is, and my general make-up and my experience have made my books shape themselves so that Calvinism could be deduced from them. I don't know; I'm not theologian enough to know. About that, or anything else.

Biles: At any rate, you are not an anti-Calvinist. You're neither Calvinist nor anti-Calvinist; you're rather eclectic about that.

Golding: Well, how can we put it? Are you for or against Fujiyama?

Biles: Yes, quite. Well said.

Golding: That's about what it is.

Biles: You've also been called, in the concern with heterodoxy, an old-fashioned Christian moralist. You *are* a moralist. In a good sense, not in a platitudinous, sanctimonious kind of way.

Golding: I think I'm a moralist, and I think there is something in the fuddy-duddy view of it that I'm a moralist in a rather objectionable sense. I find this in myself. There is *something* in that statement. Again, it's this question of patterns, and it's terribly, terribly restful to be right, terribly restful not to go ahead and say "This is good because I find it so," but to say "This is good because way back when people weren't making the mistakes"—of course, they were making mistakes—"but way back when people weren't making our kind of mistakes, this was right and so I will stand with that." That's restful, that's lazy. And there *is* something in that.

Switch from Science
to Literature

Biles: When you went up to Oxford [Brasenose College], you went there to read science, but at some point you switched from the reading of science to the reading of English literature. The question is, of course, why?

Golding: The answer is really this, that my father was a scientist, and I took from him a great admiration for science, which, in a curious way, I've still got. It took me a long time at Oxford to find that I was simply pushing a ball uphill, and I really didn't care about it.

What I really wanted to do was read what people had said. It is only now that I can turn round and see the necessity for the kind of drabness of early [*i.e.*, elementary] science. If you are going to be a scientist—which is a good thing to be, I think—you have to learn a lot of pretty dull things. You have to do a lot of biology, which seems irrelevant in many ways, et cetera. I would put it this way, that a scientist is somebody who is, as it were, working against the coal face of knowledge. He is right down in the tunnel, but it takes such a hell of a long way to get from the surface to the coal face, where the coal is. I feel, and I always have felt, when it comes to reading books—whether you take Shakespeare or Chaucer or anybody you like—that I am right up against some kind of coal face. I would want to skip all the intermediate stuff. It was, one

might almost call it, like getting into a warm bath, when I
started to read, when I found I was *officially* doing English.

Biles: How long was this from the outset?

Golding: It took two years to take the first part of my science examination, which was botany, zoology, chemistry,
and physics. It is about equivalent to your first half; it was at
Oxford in those days. I turned over and did the English thing
in two years, the same length of time. In fact, I had been
reading English when I should have been doing science.

Biles: The nominal three years for the degree you did in
two; in other words, you went along for two years, presumably working towards the science degree, and then you
chucked it.

Golding: No. I passed that [the science examination].

Biles: Yes, you passed that and then decided not to go on.
At this point, you turned around and completed the nominal
three years for the English literature degree in the next two
years. You got going great guns on the literature.

Golding: I had already been reading, and when I went to
see an English tutor, he asked what I had read. I realize now,
looking back at it, that I had read as much as many people
would have read by the time they got their degrees. This is
literally true; instead of doing my science, you see, which I
had pushed into a tiny little bit of my life, I was reading an
enormous range of literature. It wasn't all that difficult to
change over.

Biles: The truth of the matter is that you were up there
doing something, officially, that you didn't want to do and
had no business doing. All the time, you were not actually
doing it, but were reading English literature. You realized
what the case was and switched officially.

Golding: I had realized it the year before, but I thought it would hurt my father so much. I don't know that I even thought that in positive terms, but there was certainly this tremendous parental drag. And so, there it was.

And how *easy* it is to switch over and how much you very often know that people who have been in that school don't know, because they have been just going along the track, whereas you have been playing all the way around.

Biles: Well, you finally have to come back to "Home is where the heart is."

Golding: That's perfectly true.

Archaeological Background

Biles: Would you fill me in a bit on your background in archaeology? You obviously have read a sizable amount in this field, at one time or another in your life, and you have done some field work rather continuously over a long term, what one calls amateur archaeology. How did you get started in this somewhat unusual avocation?

Golding: It is difficult to say how I got into this business, because I have always been interested in it. There is no simple way of saying such a thing. I was always interested in how things were made and why. And old churches, I was always curious to know how old they were and what the people were like who built them, and so on. Of course, this is apart from Schliemann's Troy. This is really the place where archaeology did begin. . . .

Old Pitt-Rivers, who lived just over the hill there [from Ebble Thatch], was a general and he brought generalship to what was then antiquarianism and got the whole thing straightened out. He employed platoons of men and shifted hills, et cetera, and took notes of it all.

Biles: Why did he do all this? Was he an amateur archaeologist?

Golding: He was an eccentric.

Biles: Like one of those eighteenth-century fellows?

Golding: Yes. He was an eccentric. He was a most unpleasant man altogether. Well, he was an extraordinary man. About 1870, would it be, he had got interested in the bumps and ridges on his estate, and he decided he would find out what went on there. He was a general of Royal Engineers; so he knew about surveying and all the rest of it, and he simply used the same sorts of techniques. He got squads of people and laid the whole thing out and made them dig, and he kept records. The result was that the digs he did in 1880 can still be used, because it was so well recorded, even though his deductions from them were all wrong. Nowadays, people can go back to those records and see exactly what there was there and evaluate it just as though it were a modern dig. That was in 1870.

Biles: In some ways, then, he was the first to . . .

Golding: He was the first, yes. I remember, as a boy about ten [circa 1921], cycling out to Silbury Hill [the largest artificial mound in Europe, six miles west of Marlborough] and watching Pitt-Rivers with great awe. Already archaeologists were heroes of mine, for some curious reason or other. I took part in digs, and while I was at school, I ran an archaeology society, which means for about fifteen years. . . .

Biles: You mean at Bishop Wordsworth's School [in Salisbury, where Golding taught for many years]?

Golding: Yes. I was taking part in odd digs around the place. I did an awful lot of walking. Just a general interest. It's very amateur, very amateur indeed.

Biles: Your brother refers to a book entitled *Nat the Naturalist,* which he said was one of your very favorite books, that you simply read it over and over and over, when a boy. Might this interest of yours stem from *Nat the Naturalist* or some such book?

Golding: No, that was nothing to do with archaeology at all. I don't know where my interest began.

Biles: As far back as you can remember, then, the fascination has existed—from your childhood?

Golding: Yes.

Biles: According, again, to the essay about the murdered old woman, you have done something more than simply take a spade and putter about yourself.

Golding: I have taken part in digs, too. You see, the point is that this locality [Wiltshire and environs] is very, very much a kind of heart of archaeology in Britain. First of all, it has got Stonehenge just over the hill, and all that.

Mrs. Golding: The probability that you would be out stumbling over a barrow is quite strong.

Golding: I don't have to go abroad or even go to any other part of England to do archaeology, to take part in digs, and be interested in this kind of thing, 'cause it's all the way around. For example, there is a barrow up on the hill there [behind Ebble Thatch], just about a half mile away. Men up in the pub here [at Bowerchalke], the old men, used to talk about the golden boat that was hidden under it. Everybody laughed at this, until in Sweden they excavated a barrow like that and they dug up a golden boat of the sun, with a disk on it. Probably what happened here was, in the eighteenth, or even in the seventeenth, century some excavationist got this [disk] out and melted it down. The legend still goes on around here. So the whole place is very much . . . It's difficult to know where archaeology and history and ordinary life . . .

Mrs. Golding: . . . and antiquarianism . . .

Golding: . . . to know where to draw the line between them. It's that kind of neighborhood.

In addition, I have always been very much interested in architecture, in our own particular sort of architecture, like Salisbury Cathedral and that sort of thing. This is a remarkable area for such.

I don't think there is, I can't think of another area that I know anything about that would be at all like it, except, perhaps, the Delta in Egypt. Really, literally, Wiltshire is not a place so much as a kind of palimpsest of various generations and centuries. In this county you can go back to 1800 B.C. That gives you, in round terms, four thousand years of coming and going, and it has all left marks on the place; hence, you don't know whether you are dealing with an ack-ack site of the last war or an Iron Age settlement. It could be either.

Mrs. Golding: Sometimes both.

Golding: Sometimes both. If you go up to Old Sarum [north of Salisbury (New Sarum), ancient site of a British entrenched camp, a Roman station, a Saxon town, the seat of the Bishop of Sarum from 1075 to 1220 (part of the stone from Old Sarum Cathedral was used in the construction of Salisbury Cathedral)], for example, in the outer perimeter, which is, I think, Iron Age—no, it's Bronze Age—in the perimeter, you find sunk in it weapons pits from the last war, which does confuse the issue.

Mrs. Golding: With a Norman castle . . .

Golding: . . . in the middle. It is the place where William the Conqueror required the oath of allegiance. What do they call it? [By the Oath of Salisbury in August 1086 William established the principle that vows of loyalty to the sovereign took precedence over vows of loyalty to subordinate lords.] They have got one of the original copies of Magna Carta in the cathedral [at Salisbury] and this kind of thing. You just walk around here and you stub your toes over such.

Boys [at Bishop Wordsworth's School] used to keep bringing me in spearheads and things like that. One embarrassing incident I recall was that I refused to follow something up and lost the boy's name, when he had brought me one of those . . .

Mrs. Golding: Oh, yes. Not meteorite.

Golding: Yes, it was a sort of meteorite, of a special kind. Anyway, when I later saw a [meteor] chart of the world, I realized that this part of Europe was left out and a boy had actually brought me a specimen. I have no idea where he is or who he was, but it certainly was one of these.

Background for *The Spire*

Biles: Tell me about the background for *The Spire*. I know that you taught a course in church history for a time at Salisbury, but that is not directly related.

Golding: Well, honestly, there isn't any background. I know all this sounds idiotic, but consider it in this way. Incidentally, I remember Frank [Kermode] writing to me, because he was at Harvard, or somewhere up in New England, at that time and he read *The Spire* and he said what he thought about the book. He asked what my research was. He had even gone and found some book that somebody wrote. I wrote back and said I didn't do any research for this book. It is *literally* true.

The thing is, if you want chapter and verse, I can give it to you only in this way: if you have lived for half a century or more in the south of England and you are naturally curious about a great many things, one of the things you're curious about is churches. You see? I wouldn't call myself *in any way* an expert over churches, but I'm informed.

I can't remember the time when I haven't looked at churches and said to myself, "Well, now, they put a buttress there because of this, you see. And the roof can be that wide because there is this row of pillars down here," and so on. I have looked at Norman architecture and understood how they always overplayed their hand. They weren't taking any risks; everything was gorillalike. You know, in the sense of strength.

And, gradually, you get a technology, a know-how, coming along, so that you can cut away more and more stone. You really should go down there and look at the east end of Westminster Cathedral. You'll find the Henry VII Chapel, I think it is, which is practically a piece of advanced technology. It's glass and the least possible bit of stone. The whole thing is worked out to the last inch of know-how. Well, that's the transition from this kind of gripped, gorillalike strong form to this complete technical know-how.

Now I haven't read books about this; I have lived with it, and these are perfectly simple to me. *The Spire* was easy to write.

Biles: What you are saying squares with something Frank said to me, and I thought it was a very curious way of putting it. Frank said, "Oh, Bill figured out how spires were built."

Golding: That's right.

Biles: This was his phrase, "figured out." And I thought, "Now that is just like Bill."

Golding: That's the only way to do it, isn't it?

Biles: Well, no. It *isn't* the only way to do it, and it isn't the way most people would do it. It may be the only way for a man like you to do it, but you're a curious fellow. Most men would get books and they would learn about flying buttresses and lintels and architraves and the whole business I don't know anything about. But you wouldn't do that; you would stand there and set your damned stubborn head, and you'd say, "Now how did that jackass do that?" That is the way you would do it; so you say it is the only way. But it's *not* the only way; it's the only way for you.

Golding: Well, I've got to enter a caveat here. I did, I will tell you, I did look up one book. It was in the Salisbury library. It was on the statutes of the cathedral, about how many times a day they would pray and how they would behave to each other, and so on and so forth. That took three-quarters of an hour; that was my research.

Biles: In the little bit that I have been able to read of what people have said about *The Spire*, newspaper reviews and whatnot, some few of these people have apparently dug around a little and they point out that there actually was a dean named Jocelin and this kind of thing. But "Jocelin" was merely a medieval-sounding name to you?

Golding: It was not only medieval; there are still people called Jocelin. I know at least one person called Jocelin. I wanted something which would fit. I didn't really want this to be a medieval book, anyway. I didn't want it to be a historical novel.

Biles: And it isn't, either.

Golding: Well, that was what I was after.

Biles: None of your books is "historical," not even *The Inheritors*.

Golding: That's a *pre*historic book.

Biles: Is it true that the spire of Salisbury Cathedral, which is the highest spire in England, is without proper foundation?

Golding: Yes. Well, it may not be literally true, but in any case, my book doesn't necessarily have to be about Salisbury, does it? I deliberately knocked a couple of transepts off Salisbury Cathedral in order to be able to have chapter and verse for its not being.

Biles: And then you did another thing—I presume you did it—which follows from that. The dust wrapper of the third impression (1961) of *Pincher Martin* indicates "for publication in the Autumn of 1962, *Barchester Spire,*" but the title is not *Barchester Spire.* It is simply [*The*] *Spire,* and this was a moving away from localizing. Trollope's Barchester can be localized. Did you originally intend to call it *Barchester Spire?*

Golding: I did. I can't even begin to say when my interest in Salisbury spire began, because I taught under it for about twenty years; so one can't say. But I remember thinking how strange it was that Trollope could have written all these novels about the place and there is nothing in them about the cathedral at all. Really nothing in them about the thing for which the cathedral is really most preposterous—I think one can call it that—the spire, which *is* preposterous. It is rather like—what was his name?—Lloyd Wright . . .

Biles: Frank Lloyd Wright.

Golding: Frank Lloyd Wright. Rather like his setting out to erect a building a mile high. With modern technology, they might do it, but it would be that kind of preposterous thing to do. Yet Trollope, if he noticed, didn't want to write about it; he wanted to write about Mrs. Proudie and Bishop Proudie and all that. I suppose I began with an idea of writing some Barchester-like novel and the word "Barchester" got stuck as a sort of convenience. Then, afterwards, I tossed it out, because it didn't seem any longer appropriate; you would hardly know I was talking about the same place.

Biles: Originally, in this thinking that you have been describing, you had some sort of half-formulated notion of turning Trollope upside down?

Golding: No, no. I wouldn't dream of turning Trollope upside down. Trollope is one of those nice, friendly, safe people and should be left the right way up.

Biles: I agree with that.

Golding: Isn't it so? He is concerned with people in a very modest kind of social way. I won't hear a word against Trollope.

If you like, put it this way, *The Spire* in *some* ways, but not *all*, grew out of the idea that people had written books about Barchester, and I was in an ideal situation to write my book about Barchester, and it didn't really turn out to be a Barchester novel at all.

Biles: Tell me this. Everyone finds a heavy sexual imagery in *The Spire*, and somewhere I came across the suggestion that, at some point, the title for this book was proposed by you to be *The Erection.*

Golding: I really went round being cruel to publishers. I knew they would never wear this, but I said I thought this ought to be called *An Erection at Barchester.* I had a lot of fun with that.

Biles: I'm sure you did.

Golding: Mind you, nobody would ever wear it, and it's not true, anyway. It's not really the right title. The kind of diplomacy that went on with at least two of the publishers—I suppose that is two lots of publishers, American and English; they were the only two—weaned me away from this, in the kindest kind of way.

Overriding Necessity

Biles: In the essay on Copernicus, you use the phrase "the overriding human necessity of finding a link between separate phenomena," but in *Free Fall* Sammy says, "There is no bridge." I insist that, while Sammy may say there is no bridge, you yourself obviously do not believe that; otherwise, you wouldn't continue to wrestle with the split between the rational and the irrational, the scientific and the spiritual. Everything you have said about other matters—for instance, you said in New York on a television program that "No work of art can be motivated by hopelessness; the fact that people ask questions about hopelessness indicates that there is hope." And so, this overriding human necessity. Would you say anything at all about what you mean by "overriding human necessity"? Do you mean this is the most important thing in the life of man?

Golding: Yes, I think so. It's the need to have a sense of discrete, disparate phenomena on every level. I'm not thinking now of phenomena in strict philosophical terms; I'm thinking perhaps of events—I don't know—but events psychological, emotional, religious, philosophical, mystical even, scientific, whatever you like to call it—even going and fetching the milk in in the morning. It seems to me that you can't have done anything in life, if you can't put fetching the milk in in the morning into quasars and all the rest of it, into the latest of astronomy and the deepest kind of experience. The whole thing surely *has to be* a unity. If there is one faith I have, it is that there *is* a unity. And it seems to me that man hasn't seen this.

I don't know if it's lucky or unlucky, but it seems to me that what happens is that you get brought up in an apparent unity. If I, for example, had been born a Roman Catholic, that is one sort of unity; if I had been born, as it were, a Marxist, that is one sort of unity; as it happens, I wasn't born either. I don't think I was born anything in particular; so, I found myself in the chaos of existence. Well, now, I think anybody who is born into any of those systems, who lives in one of them, has, at some point, to shatter them. He may come back to them, but they've *got* to break down into this at first incomprehensible—maybe *always* incomprehensible— well, this chaos that is really what we live in, when you add the whole thing up.

It seems to me that man's—I don't know whether "business" is the word or whether man's "instinct" or what; call it "the overriding necessity" we're talking about—it seems to me that this is what he's for; in a way, this is what he *must do*. Somehow or other, he has *got to bring the whole thing together*. He may get hints here and there, and maybe he never will, I don't know, but it's a tendency. It's like the way some—most—plants crawl towards the light, no matter what. They may never get there, but they crawl, you know. And this is what I think men are for.

Biles: Now there are two or three things that occur to me and already, probably, I have incorporated these at some point. You know, the Wordsworthian idea that the poet sees unity in diversity. This is one of the things, it seems to me, that you have been saying. Another thing is Milton's idea that man was given reason—that's the thing that discriminates him from the lower animals—and there wouldn't be any point in having reason if one didn't use it. God says that Job did the right thing to inquire, so this is a part of the human. Then, a third thing, that the system—such as Catholicism or Marxism or whatever—I take it that you are saying that what is wrong with those systems is that, like rationalism, they either ignore or deny that part which their system does not comprehend.

Golding: Yes, that's about the long and short of it, I think.

Biles: That's a fair statement, then?

Golding: Yes.

Biles: Coming back to the rational-irrational now. Aldous Huxley said in that last novel of his, *Island,* "We cannot reason ourselves out of our basic irrationality. All we can do is to learn the art of being irrational in a reasonable way."

Golding: I would think this is all right for Aldous Huxley.

Biles: For Aldous Huxley, yes. But my question about this —you see, a friend of mine said to me, "Isn't it interesting that Mr. Golding in his assaults upon rationalism is sometimes so very rational about it?"

Golding: A contradiction in a way. Or is it? I think it's only another example of the fact that life experience is basically paradoxical. This is perfectly true. It becomes an infinite regression, doesn't it, that I want to destroy rationalism, so I will use rationalism to do it. I wish, for example, to promulgate religion; therefore, I will be religious or mystical about it, and these go on round, their wheels turn and go on buzzing and buzzing and buzzing. Somewhere or other, they all have got to be geared into each other.

Don't get me wrong; I don't think I'm the man to do it, mark you. I'm not even being humble here; I'm seeing the problem for the size it is. In a way, it isn't even my job, except I suppose it's everybody's job. Whether it can ever be done, I wouldn't know.

Biles: Here's a statement that I wrote, and I would like to ask you if you think this is relatively true to the case. I asserted that "The dissociation of thought and feeling"—whatever terms you want to use, this is the rational-irrational business—"has resulted in a unilateral view. The rationalist view, which ignores or denies the irrational, for example, this partial view loses sight of so much and discounts and undervalues so much of what is essential that at the worst you would get into an atheistic orientation and at the best an egocentric orientation."

Golding: Yes, I think that's a valid statement. I think it's perfectly true. This is the problem. I suppose you can only say as a footnote to that, which is a very good summation, that to be aware of that situation may possibly be, in some ways, a bit of a solution or tending towards a solution. But I'd like to say: don't credit me, the way people do all the time, with solutions. I haven't *got* them. You see, *ever*.

The Inheritors

Golding may be a writer of pessimistic books, but the man himself is an optimist.

He has said so, publicly and privately, many times. In the interview with Maurice Dolbier, printed in the New York Herald Tribune on May 20, 1962, Golding not only asserted his optimism, but also dilated upon it: "Oh, I'm an optimist. Not the naïve sort that believes civilization is getting better and better when it's obviously getting shakier and shakier. But I'm more optimistic about man than people think. I even look on him as a sort of divinity. His social structures won't cure evil; that must be done by his work on himself and his immediate surroundings. The basic point my generation discovered about man was that there was more evil in him than could be accounted for simply by social pressures."

Golding went on about the inherent wickedness of man, but spoke most optimistically about the self-sufficiency of goodness.

Golding: We all saw a hell of a lot in the war that can't be accounted for except on the basis of original evil. Man is born to sin. Set him free, and he will be a sinner, not Rousseau's "noble savage."

Interviewer: *But didn't the war also provide evidence on the other side?*

Golding: *I believe, you see, that good can look after itself; it is self-propagating. The weight of any investigation must be in asking why man commits evil, rather than why he sometimes does good.*

In response to a question about The Inheritors, *Golding continued in the same vein. In relevant part, he said, "I picture the Neanderthals as a primitive but good race that existed before the Fall, wiped out by Homo sapiens simply because it wasn't evil enough to survive. Its animal innocence was no match for our capacity for surviving at all costs. It's an odd thing—as far back as we can go in history we find that the two signs of Man are a capacity to kill and a belief in God."*

Biles: To revert to your reading in archaeology, how much *have* you read?

Golding: As far as I can remember, when I wrote *The Inheritors*—this is what this is about, isn't it?

Biles: Yes.

Golding: When I wrote *The Inheritors*, I had read about all there was to read. In fact, if you found a contradiction between Neanderthal man as he is now known and Neanderthal man as I wrote about him, my guess is you will find that it has been discovered since.

Biles: You are saying that, in a virtually literal sense, you had read all the standard works in the field.

Golding: I would say that, but equally, I'm not a professional.

Biles: Of course.

Golding: I could be caught out on this one, but I would guess my knowledge of Neanderthal man was about as wide as it could be for an amateur at that time. Let's put it that way.

Biles: I picked up a reference over here to "The Monkey People," which must be a story about Neanderthals. Do you know this?

Golding: Yes. You will find it in Wells' *Collected Short Stories.* It is a very long short. It has got a very amusing last sentence, which I will allow you to discover for yourself. It's a very funny last sentence, but the thing I disapprove of about it is that in the course of this long short story, this tormented man discovers everything except the computer. You know, it's one of those: the way you can't let go of primitive man before he has learned to build, brew beer, make fire, all the rest. Wells' man even ends up writing on the wall.

Biles: Yes. This is why Nick Furbank raised the question of the *Just So Stories.*

Golding: Oh, did he? How did he raise it, anyway?

Biles: In his review of *The Spire,* he runs briefly through all your books, and he refers very tentatively to the *Just So Stories* in connection with *The Inheritors.* I asked what he had in mind, and he mentioned the fact that some of those stories are about how things came to be made. But I couldn't remember for the life of me that your Neanderthals invent anything.

Golding: This is the great point about Neanderthals.

Biles: Exactly.

Golding: Within limits, incapable of invention. They weren't quite as uninventive as I made them, I think; I believe they did knock chips off stone and shape things a bit.

Biles: Well, you have them using stones, not actually chipping on them.

Golding: Precisely, but I think the latest information may be that they did; however, I'm not concerned.

Evil and Intelligence

Golding: I think it's perhaps an equation which I might think is no longer valid—but I'm not sure about that—an equation of intelligence with evil, a fairly straightforward equation. Therefore, the quality of innocence in Neanderthal man is a very sad thing, inseparable from ignorance; whereas, perhaps, in boys intelligence and evil are not inseparable, but parallel things, as a matter of genetics.

Biles: Are you making a distinction or an identification between intelligence and knowledge? In other words, what I have gathered along the way is that knowledge brings guilt, that knowledge and guilt equate.

Golding: Knowing what you have done here has, very likely, made a split in my thinking. I don't know that I thought as clearly as this about the distinction to be made between knowledge and intelligence. I'm not sure that I wouldn't tend to put the emphasis more on saying that intelligence and evil are inextricably mixed up, whereas knowledge and evil may not be. After all, knowledge, just because it's used in the Authorized Version, doesn't have to say that this is what we're talking about.

Biles: Well, now, we're back to Hamlet, nothing is good or bad, "but thinking makes it so." And it is the intelligence which takes the knowledge and makes it evil?

Golding: You see, Neanderthal man knew as much as Homo sapiens, in terms of knowing. He knew one flower from another, he knew one bird from another, he knew how to get in out of the rain, that there was a hole in the rock, and so on. This is knowledge, but it wasn't intelligence.

Biles: Not intelligence. This helps, because I have been bothered all along about intelligence, knowledge, and guilt. You think that guilt and intelligence equate, instead of guilt and knowledge?

Golding: I think so.

Biles: I have a memorandum here: "It takes knowledge to control nature." But I ought to have "It takes intelligence to control nature."

Golding: Oh, yes.

Biles: And intelligence involves guilt. Is the control of nature in itself sinful, guilty?

Golding: Just perhaps.

Biles: It may be, but it doesn't have to be.

Golding: Well, look at it this way: we have certainly got to the point where it is, have we not?

Biles: Yes, we have.

Golding: Whether the beginning of this is sinful, don't ask me, but what you and I as people apart from our books are stuck with is the fact that the control of nature has become sinful. And it is being controlled not through knowledge but through intelligence.

Biles: The operation of intelligence upon knowledge.

Golding: Yes.

Biles: The New People used the stag—this is a rutting stag, by the bye—in their rituals, and these people made paintings, more or less like cave paintings. When they ate Liku and buried her bones, they drew a stag on the ground and drew the red demon over it. This is a propitiatory kind of thing.

Golding: Well, they've got to the point where they've invented for themselves out of Lok and Fa this kind of devilish picture. You see, this doesn't exist at all [the painting shows the "red demon" as "in the act of some frantic cruelty"]. They've invented something which simply isn't there, but they have to make a picture of it and give it offerings. They put some meat down there and give it some drink.

Biles: The propitiation comes out of the fact that they are guilty.

Golding: True. They propitiate because they have done something they know is at the very least *against* this kind of creature; they've eaten this girl, and eating a girl is a powerful affair.

Biles: A corollary question: why are there so many homosexuals in the present-day novel? In your books, homosexuality is only hinted at once or twice. If, however, you could say that, in the contemporary novel, heterosexual sex affords the type of sin, could you also say that, perhaps, homosexual sex represents an ultimate sin, a sin beyond sin? Or, on the other hand, nothing of the sort at all?

Golding: Well, I'd have to own, with a certain amount of contrition here, that I simply don't know anything about, or understand, homosexuals. This is a literal private truth, and I would even go so far as to say that, knowing as little about it as I do, when you talk about this being a "sin beyond sin," it might conceivably be no sin at all, in my terms.

Biles: Not in Greek terms, certainly.

Golding: Yes, but there is a point coming up here: that sexual sin is exploitation of one person by another.

Biles: You mean *lust* instead of *love?*

Golding: Well, I don't know whether that is true or not. When exploitation enters into sex, it becomes sinful. Now it could possibly be, as I see it, that a homosexual love affair could have no exploitation; in which case, it would have no *sin.* Inescapably built into our society is that, at some point in heterosexual relationships, one person exploits the other; this, I think, is really true, and therefore it is sinful. It's the exploitation, not the sex.